Overcoming Con

G CHI
MAN

LS grew up in Scotland and England,
ca when she married. Returning to

Overcoming Common Problems Series

Overcoming Common Problems

Helping Children Cope with Change and Loss

Rosemary Wells

sheldon **PRESS**

Published in Great Britain in 2003 by
Sheldon Press
1 Marylebone Road
London NW1 4DU

© Rosemary Wells 2003

British Library Cataloguing-in-Publication Data

A catalogue record for this book is available from the British Library

ISBN 0–85969–891–3

1 3 5 7 9 10 8 6 4 2

Typeset by Deltatype Limited, Birkenhead, Merseyside
Printed in Great Britain by Biddles Ltd
www.biddles.co.uk

Contents

Acknowledgements

I would like to express my sincere thanks to all the people who have spent time talking with me, giving so freely of their professional advice and knowledge. In particular, I owe a great deal to Nicky Bagust, Val Haslem, Margaret Lloyd, Chris Ripley, Ruth Seymour, Jean Wills and many others for their kind interest in my research for this book. I would especially like to mention Veronica Phillips of CHASE Children's Hospice Service; Emma Maynard, Project Officer for West Sussex Young Carers Group; and Harbhajan Purewal, Carers Centre Manager for Hammersmith & Fulham Young Carers Project.

I am also very grateful to all the organizations and their teams who enabled me to study their work – including Al-Anon, Surrey Child Minding Association, Surrey Police Youth Affairs, Gingerbread, Surrey Foster Care, Bright Eyes Nanny Agency, CHASE Children's Hospice Service, Surrey Young Carers Project, Disability Information Services for Surrey, and The Children's Society.

Finally, I would like to give heartfelt thanks to all the families, especially the children, who were so kind in sharing their experiences with me.

I owe so much to them all.

Preface

Children hate change. They like stability and security in their lives. Yet how many of them get through their childhood years without having to face several small changes or large upheavals?

The causes of these disruptions are many and varied – from tragedies including illness, death and war to disasters such as fatal accidents, earthquake or flood, or domestic upheavals including divorce, moving house, or a change of school or carer.

All such changes involve loss of one kind or another, and all will alter a child's life – perhaps for ever – for loss is a cumulative experience.

Change in itself can be a cause of extreme stress. However, not all changes are tragedies – many create happiness and reinforce security for the children involved.

Even during our children's early lives, we as parents should enable our families to understand that changes – for whatever reason – are part of all our lives. How then can we help them to prepare for, and cope with, whatever life has in store for them?

When you know a change – however slight or however overwhelming – is about to occur, talk about it. Not by giving dire warnings of disasters to come, but by creating an atmosphere where family discussions can take place. You can't lessen a tragedy or hide your grief or anxiety, but you can prepare your child by telling him the truth. Unless we can provide such understanding in helping our children to deal with their emotions should a major loss occur, any further losses or changes – however trivial they may appear – will engender the same amount of grief.

In all the descriptions of families learning to cope with inevitable or unexpected changes you will find in this book, one truth emerges time and again – adequate preparation given by open discussion can alleviate a great deal of unhappiness and turmoil changes can cause. Families who talk, laugh and cry together are the ones who survive.

However, if you do not find a situation in this book that covers your particular problem, never hesitate to contact one of the many organizations that now exist throughout the British Isles to support children and their families. In the last couple of decades, there has been a marked increase in the liaison work going on between such groups – caring professionals, educational psychologists and counsellors, therapists and social workers, as well as parent and child helplines. All are supportive, and will help you to help your child. (See Sources of Help, p. 91.)

1

Causes of Change

Loss is the most frequent, and often most serious, cause of change – bereavement and divorce being the most obvious of tragic losses. The resultant changes in any child's life can be traumatic and will need understanding acknowledgement from all the adults around him.

The changes that will inevitably follow the death of a parent can bring undreamed-of problems, as can the death of a sibling – when the surviving children will feel neglected, angry and miserable all at the same time. A family death may mean a child going into care or a foster home – changes that may well exacerbate their grief. When parents divorce, their children need constantly updated and truthful explanations. Children cling to their familiar world, and suddenly this is crumbling around them – they need reassurance that their parents will still love and be in contact with them. Other changes will follow – a stepparent may come into their lives; a half-brother may be born and take a child's place as the baby of the family. Other losses, such as loss of a parent's job, can cause huge changes. Moving away from home, school and friends can result.

Compared with such overwhelming events as accidents, fires or floods, earthquakes or the consequences of a war, these changes appear far less dramatic. But to the families concerned they are the cause of great upheavals and adjustments.

As will be seen in further chapters, some children have to face horrendous changes within their own homes: older brother may take to drugs or alcohol, baby sister becomes terminally ill, Dad is in trouble with the police, the family home is reclaimed causing a move to bedsit accommodation.

Others experience happier changes: a beloved granny moves in, Dad gets a new job which means holidays overseas, a longed-for baby is born, Mum allows you to have a puppy, new stepsisters become your best friends.

As we follow the lives of many families, we shall see that all childhood losses and changes do not lead to unhappiness, but are simply part of life. And they begin earlier than any of us can remember!

Very early days

Her family is the most important part of a small child's life. Her mother, father or full-time carer, and any siblings, make up her whole world. Surely any change in her life, particularly any of those mentioned above, would only occur following a loss – the death of a parent, or the aftermath of a war which claimed her home or family?

But there are changes throughout all our lives and, such major tragedies apart, the first change for any child must be that of being weaned from breast or bottle milk to solid foods. Many childcare experts consider weaning to be an important stage in the process of a baby's developing independence. Even at three or four months old, your baby will be aware of this slight change, this slight separation, between her and her mother.

'I gave Ben his mashed-up vegetables and rice and he just spat it out!' That young mother was not the only one to experience problems with her first try at introducing what are euphemistically called 'solid' foods to her baby's diet. But a first lesson in preparing your children for the inevitable changes that are to come in their lives *can* be learned in these early days. Where change is expected, or anticipated, it is always wise to warn children of what is to come. Just as you should very gradually introduce new food to a baby, you can – as you will see in the chapters to follow – gradually introduce your children to the idea of any impending changes in their family life. This is one of the ways in which you can prepare the children – by enabling them to understand that changes are a natural part of life, that everything in life is constantly changing.

Children hate change because there is comfort in the familiar. One seven-year-old was heard to remark emphatically, 'Change is unsettling!' However, as Dr Robin Skynner writes: 'To accept change easily requires that we see it as normal, natural and necessary.' As parents we have to understand this truth and endeavour to give our children the resources to face the adjustments in day-to-day activities that small or large changes may engender.

2

The Early Years

Starting playgroup

Whether a child attends a playgroup, or any type of nursery or pre-school, is a matter of personal choice for every family. Once a decision has been made, it will usually be the first major change in a small child's life – a big step, and one that can influence his future reaction to school life. Some play-school teachers talk of this as another 'weaning' period, which describes well the separation, or weaning away, from their parent. As parents we have to remember that this is a real transition time in our child's development – they're moving from the inner world of home and family to the attractions of the outer world. We have to make sure this process is exciting and fulfilling for them and not anything to be feared. No need to make 'a big thing' of it, but just recall your own childhood and try to understand your child's emotions during this new experience.

It is worth checking with the Pre-School Learning Alliance (formerly the Pre-School Playgroup Association) for a group they recommend in your area. Many are run by qualified teachers, some by mothers in a local hall. Many parents and teachers agree this to be a happy step for little ones – 'A change in their lives is good – and good for Mum!' However, preparation for this step is essential, which means staying with your child for the first few days until he is playing happily and can be left for an hour or so at a time. Nursery school teachers tell us that a child who has attended a playgroup, or pre-nursery school, takes more readily to the next step.

Margaret felt that her daughter had no need for such a step. 'She has two sisters and two brothers, and is used to playing with others.' But when little Janey came to playgroup and met others of exactly her age, she was not used to being confronted by her rather demanding peers! 'I realized that her brothers had always given in to her, and her sisters were younger than her and never bothered her, so she was used to having her own way! At playgroup she learned to share her toys – I'm glad I let her go.'

Nursery school

These schools are run by the educational authority with roughly the same length of terms and hours as primary schools. Although they meet many early educational needs, they are not for formal learning. As one teacher said, 'A good nursery school is a complement to school, never a substitute.' Happily, these schools do not have to follow the National Curriculum, although in the final year children could be gradually introduced to a Literacy Hour and a Numeracy Hour. Instead, nursery schools follow a different strategy, known as a Foundation Document. This means that there is no compulsion, no stress, and children have time to learn social skills alongside some elementary educational lessons. Nursery schools accept children from the age of three, although some parents choose to keep their children either at home or at a playgroup until they reach the compulsory school age, which is younger in Britain than in most countries throughout the world. Many primary schools now have nursery school departments, which means that the children are well acquainted with their surroundings when the time comes for them to attend full-time schooling.

Most nursery school teachers are supportive in their methods of introduction to the new surroundings. Some welcome parents as far as the door of the classroom, others encourage parents to stay with their child for the first few sessions so that he or she can get to know and trust one special teacher or helper. This is what the well-known child psychologist John Bowlby called 'forming an attachment'. Once the child has achieved this and has come to trust the teacher, the parent can safely 'detach' from the situation. Co-operation with the teacher is all-important in this process, but it is up to the parent to prepare the child for some time beforehand, so that the separation is gradual and enjoyable for parent and child. For remember, your little child's relationship with you will inevitably alter. She will have to be more independent. If she is an only child, then it is wise to invite friends around, so that she becomes used to playing with others, to sharing her toys and not being with adults most of the day.

What else can and should parents do? Don't be like Mary Ann, who tried too hard to prepare her poor child for this new venture. 'I worried about this big change, so I taught him to count to a hundred, he can read easy words, he knows all the colours of the rainbow and

4

the days of the week.' But could her brilliant offspring button his own coat or find his own way to the toilet? Any teacher will tell you how unfair it is to her, and indeed to the child, if he is unable to perform such simple tasks. Happily for mothers and teachers today, most children's shoes have Velcro fastenings rather than laces!

These practical preparations aside, it is a wise parent who will take her child to the nursery, perhaps the term before he is to start, so that he is familiar with the journey, whether on foot or by car or bus. And do make the whole change into a happy one – a new adventure, one that your child feels he is lucky to be entering into. Of course, children, maybe in the same family, all react differently. Most do accept this first away-from-home experience quite happily, but others find it difficult and will cry, plead a tummyache, or feel – sometimes actually be – sick. A small child clinging to your legs, refusing to let go of your hand, and crying as you wave goodbye, reduces most mums to tears themselves – an agony they never forget. Even when the teacher assures you later that your child's tears began to dry as soon as you were out of sight, you still feel you have failed in preparing your little darling. Experience has shown that on leaving a child at nursery, there is no need for a prolonged farewell as if you are going on a holiday for three months! Much better not to linger, but to go as if you mean to come back. It is impossible to explain why some children tend to be more anxious than others – it will require patience and understanding and a genuine rapport with the teacher. Then, once your child begins to form friendships with other children as well as her teacher, mornings will soon become a pleasure for you both.

It must also be remembered that many children, especially the first child in a family to attend school, do not always appreciate that it is an ongoing arrangement. It is not just an 'outing', as Darren thought. He enjoyed the first day, but was amazed when his mother expected him to attend again. 'I've been to school,' he said indignantly. Another little boy was bitterly disappointed when the teacher instructed each child to answer with the word 'Present' when his name was called. 'And she never gave me a present!' he grumbled to his mother at the end of the day.

Staying to school dinner

Another change in a child's day will come when she stays for dinner. Maybe the choice will be between taking a lunch box or being served with a meal provided by the school. Again, preparation for this new step is essential. Many youngsters arrive never having had to sit formally at a table for their meals, and some have never used cutlery before. They may also have to carry their own tray with their food to the table – quite a task. If your child is a fussy eater or has any allergies, the school must be notified. Children should be warned that meals may not be cooked in quite the same way as mum's. 'Why do we have sauce on our fish fingers?' was Angela's worried cry after her first school dinner. But Wendy was even more upset: 'Miss wasn't there, it was a strange dinner lady who didn't know my name!'

We forget that once we all had similar little worries and laugh at our children's stories. But at the time they can be genuinely upsetting, and as such must be discussed at home. Today, most schools appreciate this and do not insist on all food being finished, nor do they ever say, 'No pudding until you've eaten the first course'. They recognize the anxieties, and prefer dinnertime to be part of the teaching of social skills.

Conversely, one young boy, obviously used to eating out with his parents, was quite excited by his first school meal. 'It's just like a restaurant!' he exclaimed.

Junior school

'Big' or 'proper' school is a new world – even after nursery school or playgroup. There is more discipline, more structure to each day, and class sizes may be larger. However, your child is now used to being away from home for several hours during the day, so this new venture is more of a transition than a real change. Again, many reception class teachers will liaise with the parents to ensure any problems are ironed out as soon as possible. Several little playgroup friends may well be starting school together, which makes it all less of an ordeal. Most children love the idea of wearing a uniform – they feel more 'grown-up' and feel superior to their younger siblings still in 'home clothes'.

Even if he is used to attending nursery school, during his first term a child will be very tired on coming home – and that often means being either unusually quiet and uncommunicative or wildly noisy and boisterous. Either way, he is simply sleepy, and patience will be needed – plus a few early bedtimes! Never worry if your child becomes bad tempered or sullen and says, 'Nothing!' on being asked what the day held – he may be trying to separate his two worlds.

From now on, your child's teacher will become part of her life – many a little one will address her teacher as 'Mummy'. And Teacher's word can become law! 'Miss said that I can wear my trainers for gym if I want to – so why did you say I can't?' In such small matters, it is as well to let Teacher win the day! Naturally, in more serious situations a quick discussion with Miss will keep everyone happy. Perhaps this can be an early lesson for children in understanding that everyone has different opinions and ideas.

A notable difference now children are in primary school is that the teachers, however caring and experienced, have to work to the National Curriculum and the work accomplished is all-important.

A change of teacher can be a big trauma for some sensitive children, almost as bad as a change of carer. Teachers are usually aware of this, but parents are not always so understanding when their child suddenly refuses school.

How to help your child

The best way to ensure that your child settles happily in any new environment is to give her confidence. Let her be aware of any potential talents she has by showing enthusiasm in all her interests. Encourage any capabilities she shows – without making her arrogant, of course! Many child specialists stress that the most important thing you can teach children is independence, knowing how to stand up for themselves, in the sure knowledge that you have complete trust in them. I have seen parents drive their car up to the school gates, then lean over to open the back door to let the child out, *without even looking at the child.* They may argue that they have prepared her well, that she is not going to cry being left at school – but I would rather see the mother who gives her child a quick hug and waves goodbye. Both children may well have learned to be independent, but as a teacher, I know which child will have the most confidence in herself.

If there is a younger child at home, it is worth noting that he can also be affected by this change in the family routine. His brother or sister won't be there to play with him all the time now – he may have all the toys to himself, but he will miss the companionship. Gail remembers seeing her sister crying one morning on her way to school. 'This upset me. I wondered if I would cry when it was my turn to go.'

A new baby in the house

Just as a child is reaching the age when the beginnings of independence are growing, and she is longing to tell her parents about all her new experiences and friends at school or playgroup, her mother may well be absorbed in a new baby. This dramatic change is quite a challenge to a little girl who has always had two loving parents to herself. However well you prepare her for the new arrival and let her help in the preparation of the baby's room, she will inevitably feel some resentment, if not jealousy. Her after-school chatter, her new interests and ideas, will have to be listened to with special care. Jane, the kindest of mothers, knew that her three-year-old Lucy was excited about the arrival of a baby brother, but was shattered when she first began to breast-feed him. 'Lucy suddenly rushed at me, and tried to pull the baby away from me. It wasn't as if I hadn't told her what to expect – I was terribly upset.' It was quite some while before Lucy could be allowed into the room at feeding time, so did this make the situation worse? 'I had given her a doll, which I thought would make her feel motherly – but that hadn't worked! Then I had some wise advice from my midwife,' said Jane. 'She suggested I give Lucy her meals at the same time as the baby, with her sitting beside me with a tray on her lap. For a few days she was angrily silent, but she soon accepted the situation and refused to eat her meals anywhere else! We give her as much extra attention and love as we can while still showing her how much we all love both our children.' Jane laughed: 'The other day Lucy even told her granny that she must love the baby as much as she loved her!'

Mum goes back to work

Whether your child is three months or three years old when you decide to return to work, preparing him for this change in the household is vital. Even if you have been able to leave him with baby-sitters, grandparents or friends on many occasions, so that he trusts you always to return, that is not the same as leaving him all day, every day of the week. Now a decision has to be made, depending on your child's age (and probably your income!) – day nursery, playgroup, child minder, au pair, or nanny?

A wise move is to contact the Children's Information Services in your area. They will give you a list of all the choices, and where places are available in the various groups.

Day nurseries

These are usually run under the auspices of the local health authority – and have flexible hours to suit working parents. Many incorporate crèche facilities, although these are only intended for short-stay, temporary occasions, perhaps while a parent is shopping.

We have talked about how children, as soon as they are old enough to understand, must be introduced gradually into a playgroup or nursery school. But if you are setting off for work as soon as they have been dropped off at the school, they must know where you are going to be during the day. As soon as they are old enough to understand, tell them where you are going, and why, and how long you will be there each day, and if someone else, a friend or a daytime carer, will be fetching them.

A playgroup helper told me that the most clinging children, those who constantly look anxious and restless, unable to settle to any activity, have not been told why they are there and not at home. A surprising number of parents never realize how disturbed children can be when not given information. 'They are too young to understand, it doesn't bother them,' is a frequent excuse, but older children express such feelings for themselves. 'My mum never told us anything about her day,' said six-year-old Keith, 'yet she kept asking us what we'd been doing!'

Professional child minders

Gone are the days when Granny, Auntie or another close relative was always ready to step in if Mum had to be away. Granny may well be working herself, or living in another country; many families are isolated as far as relations are concerned. Even neighbours today do not always make up the close communities which used to make child minders unnecessary. All too often throughout the western world, this means that the emotional and comforting stability of family life enjoyed by their grandparents is lacking for our children today. So the choice of childcare is all-important.

Now that 72 per cent of mothers are working in Britain today, this is obviously a profession rapidly gaining importance. In 1977 the National Childminding Association was formed, and there are now training courses for child minders. It is optional whether a minder joins the Association, but it is a wise move, for they then get a Start-up Grant which includes insurance cover. All minders have to undergo a minimum of four hours' training, and may start work within six months of registration. Although they are termed as self-employed, since the 1989 Children Act each local authority has a legal duty to register child minders, and Ofsted carry out inspections of premises once a year – with powers to cancel a registration. There is also a requirement to have the same amount of medical knowledge as the child's parent. For example, if a child has a specific medical condition, perhaps diabetes, then the minder will be fully aware of the necessary diet. The usual first-aid certificate is wise but not essential – it is more fitting to acquire a certificate of 12-hour emergency aid for babies and young children.

In most cases, a family will negotiate with the minder as to terms, hours, etc. It is so important that the parent and the carer have a rapport with one another. As one professional wrote: 'There is a tight-rope to be walked . . . when the mother wants her child to trust and love the Minder, but feels jealous at times – as does the Minder.' It is wise to have a written contract to formalize your agreement – a safer and happier arrangement for both parties.

It is one profession where true dedication, true love of children, is essential. This is confirmed when you hear of minders who become foster parents. For such a responsible job the pay is low, ranging on average from £2.50 to £5.50 an hour. This may well be why it is extremely rare to hear of an irresponsible minder! The hours, though flexible, are often long – some parents leave a child as early as 6 a.m. if they commute a long distance to work, not fetching the child until 6 or 7 p.m. This may involve the minder in taking older children to school and fetching them again in the afternoon. Minders are not supposed to cook for the children (in order not to spend time in the kitchen), but they supervise their sandwich lunches or perhaps just heat up a dish provided by the parents. The average age of a child minder is between 30 and 45, women who have their own children in school, although they are eligible from age 18, and some older women whose families have left home make excellent minders. A few men are registered, although they usually have wives or partners who work with them.

For parents, it can be a happy choice. Your child will be living in a home atmosphere, and will also receive more consistency of care than in many day nurseries (most minders stay in work for a minimum of six years). As one child minder of twenty years' standing says, 'Child minding is a personal and flexible service.' She likes to visit the children's own home before they come to her, to see the sort of life they normally lead. She does not write notes on a child's behaviour or activities during each day, as happens in a nursery. 'I like to be with the children, not writing about them! If one child is on his own, we can go for walks, or for a bus ride. All of them get to know the neighbours, and my own children accept them as family.' All this is surely a more natural environment than a nursery can provide. Natasha, who leaves her three-year-old son with a minder who also cared for her older child before he went to school, says: 'Childcare books give a list of all the things you should ask a child minder, but it amazed me. I just knew when I met my children's minder and saw her home that it would be suitable. I have had no second thoughts.'

Childcare in your own home

If you wish your child to be looked after in your own home, then you will have to consider an au pair or a nanny.

Au pairs

The title could really be applied to a mother's help. A great many au pairs in Britain come from overseas, and take a position for six months or a year in order to learn the language and to work for a few hours a week in return for board and lodging. They are not trained child minders or nannies, and should never be expected, or asked, to look after babies. However, for older children, and for mothers who need an extra pair of hands, they can be a great success. 'My family all adored our New Zealand au pair, and she is still a friend although it is many years since she left us.' There are agencies who cater for au pairs – but do remember to check all references yourself: the girls (the vast majority *are* girls) may not expect you to check those from overseas!

Once you have found a dependable and well-recommended au pair, they will need your support during these early days. Let them see that you are not going to make excuses for your child's behaviour! Depending on the age of the child, explain that the carer is there to help and look after him; tell him firmly that she doesn't deserve to be treated unkindly.

Nannies
Surprisingly, you do not need a licence to set up a nanny agency! So it is wise to use a reliable one recommended by friends, your doctor or your health visitor. Obviously, a good agency will always meet the nannies, never put them on their lists over the phone, and of course check all references thoroughly. However, since April 2002, a new service has been in operation to give far greater peace of mind to agencies and, of course, to parents. This is Disclosure – which has been provided by the Criminal Records Bureau, an executive agency of the Home Office. Disclosure holds records of information from police, health and education departments. (There is even an Enhanced Disclosure specifically for nannies.) At the time of writing, it is not compulsory for agencies or parents to use a Disclosure check, but it would be sensible to confirm with any agency that they are using this system, or to apply for an application form yourself. This is not expensive, but surely worthwhile when searching for a person who will be responsible for the care of your child. (See Sources of Help, p. 91.)

You may well wish to interview several nannies in your own home, and this is wise. As one agency manager says: 'There must be an instant rapport between parent and nanny – if you feel uncertain, don't rush into employing them. You will usually know if she is going to fit into your family life.' Most nannies train for two years to obtain their NNEB certificate, possibly at their local technical college. (A few Australian and New Zealand girls have also received excellent training in their own countries.) Some young school-leavers become assistants at a day nursery from where they can take day release for training. Most girls are in their mid-twenties, although a few older nannies return to work after their own children leave school.

The families pay commission to the agency, who will recommend the local rates of pay and suggest terms for a contract, such as the amount of sick pay, annual holidays, reasons for dismissal, petrol allowance, etc., but it is up to the family and the nanny to arrange details between them. Most nannies live in and, naturally, are well paid, for theirs is a responsible job – they may well have a baby to look after, have more than one child to care for, work long hours and often be in sole charge for a weekend or longer.

If you want your child looked after in your home and can afford such qualified help, there are many advantages. She will be in familiar surroundings (we've seen how children hate change) and if she is sick or has a cold there is no awful decision to be made about taking her out to nursery or child minder. Also, for working mothers there is not that terrifying rush to get the child to nursery on time, or a worse race home in the rush hour to pick her up! It can certainly afford much peace of mind to a working mother. But against that, it can be a lonely life for a nanny, and perhaps for an only child, although nannies usually meet others in the neighbourhood so they and the children can get together.

However happily settled your child and her nanny may be, child psychologists advise that you always make sure your child knows where you are and when you will be coming home – the same as when she was at nursery school – and that now she also knows where to contact you at work.

Saying goodbye

Whichever form of home childcare you choose, you know that it is not permanent. Au pairs do not usually stay longer than six months or a year, and even trained nannies do not stay for generations as they used to in our grandparents' day, which in itself can cause fairly dramatic changes.

This is when a child who has been brought up to accept change as part of life will be ready to face the prospect of a trusted carer saying goodbye and a new adult coming into his life – however hard that may sometimes be. And it has been professionally noted that a child who has a strong bond with his mother will always cope more easily with changes in other relationships. Close attachments to his extended family – cousins, grandparents, and so on – can also give your child a strong feeling of permanence.

However, a nanny or au pair may have become an important part of your child's life, particularly if both his parents are away from home every day. This is one occasion when your having given your child the emotional resources to face change, and the ability to deal with it, will pay dividends. If you can treat one nanny leaving and a new one arriving more as a transition than as a dramatic change, your child will settle far more quickly and happily.

Donna was a responsible, loving mother, and when her little girl's nanny was leaving after nearly a year, she did not want the child to be sad. So she sent her to her granny for a long weekend, and installed the new nanny while she was away. 'It seemed the kindest way to handle the situation,' she said afterwards. But the little girl was devastated. 'I hate you!' was all she kept saying to the new, very able and friendly nanny. It took many months before the little girl would respond in any way to the newcomer. Donna now knows how badly she dealt with the transition. 'My sister told me how well her little boy coped when his au pair left – she's taught me such a lot.'

Donna's sister had warned her son some time before the beloved au pair had to leave and he was told he could telephone and write to her whenever he wanted. She didn't make too much of it, but explained why the girl was leaving and where she was going. His mother helped him choose a leaving present for the au pair, who in return gave him a large colouring book and a box of paints. Leaving day was sad, but not a sort of dramatic 'I'll-never-see-you-again' sort of day. Usually it is possible to arrange for the leaving nanny to overlap a few days with the new one, which enables a child to see them together – an easier transition for him to understand.

Any nanny or carer will tell you that many children, however well prepared, may resent them and be difficult and uncooperative. 'You are so stupid!' shouted one three-year-old to a very young nanny. It was several weeks before the two became friends.

Many professional psychotherapists agree that being exposed to lots of new people can be stimulating for all children. Too closeted a life will prevent them from becoming adaptable to the inevitable changes and transitions they will have to face.

3

On the Move

We've looked at children moving into their primary schools – most settling happily – so can they and their parents assume the next step up to senior school will be easy? Parents see no need for the careful preparations they gave the children to help them attend nursery, then primary school. 'They know their way around now – they enjoy school.' Their children, in Year 6 at junior school, are full of self-confidence. 'We're the top of the school – we can do what we like!' I've heard said many times by 11-year-olds.

But they are all in for a shock. Come September, they head off for Year 7 in that big school down the road and they are no longer at the top of anything! This is one move they are really going to notice, involving many changes. They may have friends who have moved with them, but they will still feel lonely and lost – in much larger, strange buildings with a bewildering number of strange children and teachers. One huge change will be that instead of one familiar form teacher, who knows them and their families well, they will have a different teacher for every subject. This will entail moving from lesson to lesson – and woe betide them if they forget to take the right books with them. They will have a new and complicated timetable. The sense of security and familiarity they felt at their old school will have gone, and as they lose their way around this new building they can suffer severe stress. Many begin to lose self-confidence, and this may well show up in their work, which often digresses in that important first year. For this is the year when the children are sorted out by their abilities, and this alone can make them feel inadequate, and perhaps inferior to their peers. They now have to learn to accept certain responsibilities, one of which may be tackling public transport on their own for the first time, so that anxiety can set in before the school day has begun. Once at school, a child may be given choices of subject – which is a huge change from his old school. 'I was asked which language I wanted to take!' said Ben, 'and then the list of extra-curricular subjects was amazing. I couldn't decide whether to join the drama club or the swimming evening, do an extra language or take guitar lessons – it was up to me!'

Happily, some primary and senior schools do liaise with each other and arrange for Year 6 classes to visit the 'big' school several times during their last term to get used to the atmosphere, perhaps watching a football game or listening to a singing lesson. Some schools lay on a two-week Summer School during the holidays which some children from Year 6 can attend to get to know the daily routine and learn their way around.

Parents, too, can help their children during this transition period. One father remembered his own schooldays. 'I recall the shock of big school – the noise, the scary changing rooms, the bullies, and not knowing any of the teachers properly. I didn't want my sons to experience that without warning. So I tended to tell them the worst things I remembered as well as the fun!' He had the right idea – and as long as parents remember that their children will be exhausted each evening, and will need support rather than criticism and a genuine interest taken in their work, they may save them from falling too far behind in class or even playing truant. As one head teacher told me: 'Parents who come to all their child's school events are very welcome. Some of them feel that they must keep well away now that their children are older, but we like them to get as involved as possible. That way we can all work as a team, and the children will benefit.' For, remember, it is just at the time, aged 11, when puberty is setting in (see Chapter 6) and their emotional and intellectual awareness is growing fast, and this important transition is more difficult than many families anticipate. But if well handled, it can be one experience that really can help children to face all the changes ahead.

Moving house

Moving house can be fun. It can also be traumatic, and is even listed among the top ten stress factors for adults. So how does it affect children? Parents sometimes forget, or simply do not realize, how conservative, i.e. distrustful of change, their children can be. After all, a child experiences a huge sense of loss when she has to leave the familiarity of her home. This is when a child's age is important – once they have started school, made friends and have a regular routine, it is hard, and as teenagers it can be really difficult. I overheard a 16-year-old say, 'If Mum moves house again, I'm leaving home!' They must be told the cause for the move – is it due to Dad's new job, Mum's remarriage, or an illness that requires treatment overseas?

A common cause is loss of income, and children today seldom take kindly to being 'different' from their friends. Change can alienate a child from his peers. Change to a new school, in a new neighbourhood, is not always easy. But if your child can be encouraged to enjoy a challenge he may settle down well. However, this is a classic case of one change leading to several more – how many more will depend on the distance involved in the move.

For the very young, even a 'sleepover' with friends is not always the fun that it sounds, and on holiday it is not always easy sleeping 'in a strange bed in a strange room'. But although it need not be traumatic, it can be bewildering. Three-year-old Nicola's mother told her they were moving to a new home nearer to the park. 'We shall have to buy some new things as it is a bigger house,' she said. Nicola, very excited, enquired, 'Will I have to buy a new toothbrush?' Aged four, Ben began behaving in a clinging and unusually babyish manner, following his mother round the house rather like a family pet when it senses you are going on holiday. His parents had not explained to him why and when they were moving. Once he was told, and shown the new home, he began to enjoy the packing up and couldn't wait for moving day. Pamela also found it fun, when her family moved only two streets away. 'Mummy took lots of books in Dad's wheelbarrow, and she let me push my toys along in the baby's pram.'

Those children were lucky, but for Tessa her family's move was to be more traumatic – it certainly seemed so to her at the time. Her father's job was taking them hundreds of miles away and this would mean many losses – notably her school and her friends. 'I don't want to leave this house, I was born here. I love my school and I want to stay here for ever!'

When they reached the new town, Tessa was inconsolable. She stubbornly refused to take any interest in the new house or her new room. 'This isn't *my* home!' she cried.

'I had no choice,' her dad explained. 'If I'd turned down this job I would have been out of work.'

'I wouldn't have cared!' Tessa refused to listen to reason.

For her mother, struggling to settle into a new neighbourhood herself, it was a nightmare. The new school were welcoming, but the 11-year-old Tessa was unsmiling and critical of everything. 'It's a horrid uniform, the kids are stupid, the teachers are boring – I hate it!'

The first term saw no improvement. Then, in the holidays, Tessa's mother met one of the teachers at the supermarket, and the teacher asked her to bring Tessa round to meet her children. Reluctantly, the girl went along, and to her surprise found that the teacher's son and daughter were also new to the town. 'Our mum and dad have split up, and Dad stayed in our old home in Wales, and Mum found a job up here. They both talked about it with us, and gave us the choice of staying at our old school, but we wanted Mum to be happy, so we came too. It's not so bad when you get to know it – some of the kids are great.' Tessa thought about her new friends, and realized how lucky she was not to have had to choose between her parents. If they could cope with such a huge change in their lives, she could cope with a change of school. After all, her parents had warned her there might be other moves in the future – but at least all three of them would be together.

There are, of course, endless reasons for a family moving house – some exciting, others upsetting – and many come about following a divorce. When Cynthia's violent husband left her, she had to leave her home and rent two rooms in a tower block. 'Strangely, the change did not seem too dramatic at the time. The children were so upset by the divorce and its consequences that the move was just one small part of the whole trauma.' When they finally moved to a house again, it was a significant landmark for the children. 'They obviously felt secure again – the house represented the stability they had lost.'

Many family moves, at home or overseas, involve a complete change of lifestyle. When Lynne's father was given a high-powered job in the City, the whole family had to leave their modest semi-detached house on the outskirts of Birmingham and move to a large apartment in London. 'We all thought how grand it looked when we arrived, but it was not very friendly. The other tenants hardly spoke to us, but we were used to all our neighbours chatting all the time, and we hated it. School wasn't too bad, as there were lots of children who didn't come from London originally, but city life was not for us. We used to beg Dad to let us go and stay with friends at home up north in the holidays.'

Most children never feel truly at home again after a sudden change in their lives. Jill remembers when her father lost his job with no warning and the family had to move into a small flat. 'We had lived in a four-bedroom house in a quiet suburb and now we were stuck in this sixth-floor flat with only two rooms and a shared bathroom. My brother and I hated it and my mum was so miserable she didn't really help us. The other kids in the block teased us when we wore tidy clothes, and our old friends wouldn't come and see us. One of the worst things was not being allowed our dog – we had to give him to our old neighbours and I cried more about that than anything.'

Such emotions can be partly due to loss of self-esteem and must be treated as seriously as any deep sadness.

Conversely, Linda and her family moved from a run-down estate in the city to a large house in the country. 'Everyone thought we had won the Lottery, but Dad had been left a lot of money. At first it was exciting,' said 14-year-old Judy. 'But we lost our city friends and had to go to a different school and were terribly lonely. Then Mum had a breakdown – I suppose it was the sudden pressure of a new life, though I guess she missed her friends too.' None of them had been prepared for the sense of loss that would follow what outsiders saw as a happy change in their lives. Perhaps adults assume that a move will not disturb adolescents so deeply as their younger children. But this is seldom the case. At a time when their friends have become a large part of their lives, to lose them is to lose something to hang on to as they face adulthood. They can feel desperately alone. Even when they leave for work or college, it can be comforting to know their old familiar home is still there.

Faraway places

A more drastic change for any family is a move to a new country. The children must be told the reasons for the move and, if time allows, be helped to say goodbyes and to make arrangements for keeping in contact with friends. It is essential they have some knowledge of the new country and its people, and are made aware of the advantages and enjoyment they will experience. It is one time when togetherness within a family is so important – so that the move can be looked on as a family adventure, rather than a tough assignment forced upon the children by their parents. It is worth noting that, however hard such a change in their lives may be for children, they are often the ones to make friends first – and to learn a new language the fastest. And in many parts of the world today it is often found that children deal far better with sectarian and ethnic divisions than most adults. Obviously, a new school will emphasize the differences in culture, language and customs.

Initially, such moves are not always happy or satisfying ones. For Phil and Dan, the losses involved were enormous. Aged 10 and 12, they were to lose contact with their friends, their school, their whole way of life in South Africa. How would they cope in a cold grey town in the heart of Scotland? 'We had to leave our dogs behind, too,' said Phil. 'We miss them lots.'

'Even though they met up with some cousins and had been told what to expect, it took them over a year to settle down,' said their mother. 'We had warned them of the weather and the different teaching methods at school, but they tended to grumble about almost everything for the first term!' However, when they saw snow for the first time, and made new friends while tobogganing, life became easier – Dan even admitted that a school outing to a mountain loch was 'cool, man!'

When Liam and his two brothers moved to northern Italy with their parents, they were told that it would all be exciting and that they would enjoy farm life. Their dad said he had always dreamed of the life. 'You boys will love it!' he told them. But Liam said they had not really any idea what to expect.

'At first, it seemed like a fun sort of holiday, but we soon began to miss England and our town life. There were no shops near us, no cinemas or anything, and when we were sent to school it meant a long drive in a jeep. It was horrid, as no one, not even the teacher, could speak any English.' Liam's mother was also beginning to feel homesick, and not being able to help them with their Italian lessons she decided to let them stay at home so they could all learn together from videos.

'This was boring, and so we found some boys on a farm near us and began to talk with them – somehow we picked up Italian and they picked up English! After that Dad said we'd better go back to school. Suddenly it all became quite fun, as the other kids were very friendly, and now we visit their homes and they come to us.' Liam laughed. 'We're teaching Mum Italian now!'

For Mary and her sisters, such changes were not unusual. Their father's work involved many moves, all over the world. 'We got used to moving. I've been to about 15 different schools,' said Mary. 'Sometimes I was sad to leave friends, but as our family was always together, it somehow seemed that we were at home wherever we went.'

Unlike Phil and Dan, who settled fairly quickly into new ways of living and learning, some children find it very hard. Such famous families as the Durrells, whose mother moved to Corfu with her young family, have found happiness and success in very different surroundings to their original towns and villages in Britain. In most cases, the changes have been appreciated – the sunshine of Australia, the wildlife of Africa, the fascinating places in the Far East – and children have taken to their new lives with ease. But there are many who found the sudden transition from their old routine difficult. 'Dad and Mum never told us we would have such odd food, or have to wear short trousers to school, or sleep in tents.'

A change of school

As we've seen, moving house often means moving school, and when this occurs during term time it can be very hard for a child – at whatever age. Not only will the surroundings be strange so that you lose your way around, but there will be a sea of new faces – and, worst of all, you will be the only child who is new in your class. However welcoming the teacher is, and often he will assign another child to help you find your way around for the first few days, it will all be bewildering. The other children will have formed their friendships, and playtime can be as daunting as lesson time.

When possible, if parents can move at the end of the school year, or at least the end of a term, it will make a huge difference to their children. Some parents are so keen not to disrupt a child's schooling – especially during their exam years – that they will allow them to stay at their old school, even if it means a longer car or bus journey every day. Other children are moved many times, simply so as not to inconvenience the parents.

When a move is unavoidable, the same methods of easing the break as those used when a nanny leaves can be applied. Let your child give his class teacher a goodbye present, and be sure he has the addresses of his special friends so that he can keep in touch – at least until he forms new friendships.

For some children, their many moves deny them much hope of firm friendships, and once they reach school age the friends in their peer group become an increasingly important part of their lives. For teenagers, loss of their friends can be far more devastating than loss of their home.

Boarding school

Parents have been known to send their children to boarding school while divorce proceedings were going on. 'It will be happier for them to be right away from all the trauma.' But unless this has been discussed and agreed upon long before any family troubles began, such a huge change could be extremely upsetting for any child. Being sent away from home will feel like a double rejection. Other parents have simply told their children that 'We went to boarding school, so you are going too – we know you'll love it.' Yes, the schools may have given them a sort of stability during their growing-up years, but they surely lost out on family togetherness. Whatever the reason, do discuss the idea with your child. Many will dread the experience, although some will find the security and stability of a school comforting after too many family quarrels or endless moves. One 12-year-old voiced the opinion of many children: 'At least we got to stay in the same school during our parents' constant moving of homes.'

There are occasions when it is necessary for a child to board at school – and, of course, schools are not the Dickensian institutions they used to be! Many children enjoy the companionship and form life-long friendships. Others, such as David, do have reservations. 'I suppose I learned to be independent,' he said. 'But in a way at boarding school you are not really independent – it's a bit like being in the Army or something – everything is arranged for you, you don't have to make many decisions for yourself. However,' he added, 'you are used to being away from home and so going to college is not so hard.'

As with all such major decisions, so long as all the pros and cons are openly discussed within the family and the children are well prepared for the move, it may well be one of those happy rather than traumatic changes.

Evacuated children

For thousands of children in Britain during the Second World War, their lives were full of changes. Sudden unavoidable moves were not unusual. Fathers and brothers suddenly disappeared, holidays were unheard of, and many spent all their nights in air-raid shelters. 'We left the shelter one morning to go home and found it had been bombed. Our whole street was just a mass of rubble. We had to live in our school hall and were given clothes by kind ladies, and life was never the same again!' A sad but not unique memory.

Many children were moved out of cities to stay with relatives and friends in the supposed safety of country areas. But for others there were no kindly aunts or uncles to welcome them. Old wartime photographs often show long lines of children, gas masks slung round their necks and little cases and carrier bags clutched in their hands, ready to board trains and buses to take them away from their families. And what enormous changes some of them suffered. New surroundings, new schools, and with no knowledge of when they would return home. For many, of course, it was not all misery. Some went with brothers and sisters so that they did not feel so alone, and many went to kindly homeowners who did their best to help them to settle down.

A less traumatic change for children came when their whole school was evacuated – as many were. Angela, aged 14, went with her London grammar school when it moved to Norfolk. 'All the staff moved with us, and we were allowed to have younger brothers and sisters, too, so my ten-year-old sister came with me. She was sent to a local village school. It was quite a responsibility having her with me. We were billeted in nearby villages, and went to school by bus each day. We were in a large detached house, with a garden. That was a big change from our London flat. We picked our vegetables from the garden. I learned how good fresh carrots tasted, and how asparagus grew! On our half-days we were entertained in the church hall, but at weekends we were left to our own devices. Out of boredom, I would go to three different churches on Sundays, with the result I never went at all when I got home. We were sent home in the holidays, so in a way it was like going to boarding school.'

Foster homes

As we shall see in further chapters, family moves are most often caused by a death, divorce or separation in a family. Upsets such as these can result in children being placed in the care of their local authority – which could mean being in residential care, in short-term fostering, or in hospital to be near a sick parent – often temporarily, because a relation could not afford to keep them. They are constantly moving – either between their parents' two homes or from one foster home to another.

For Jonathan and his family, the changes and moves involved in their lives when their mother died were devastating. They had no grandparents in the country, and were sent to foster homes. 'My brother and I went to quite a nice lady but she didn't have much time for us as she had two children of her own, and the worst thing was our little sister was sent by herself to another foster home!' Although the foster mother was kind to their sister, the child missed her brothers terribly. 'It was as if I'd lost my whole family, not just my mother.'

For 11-year-old Katy and eight-year-old Kevin, the changes in their lives were frightening when both their parents died in a car crash. 'Somehow that time of my life seemed such a sort of muddle and a cloud, I can't always remember clearly exactly what went on,' said Katy. 'We had no relations in this country, and a friend of my mum's came to stay for a few weeks. She was helpful, but had a family of her own and had to leave. I think our neighbours came round for a bit, but then Social Services seemed to take over. We had to go to foster homes, but for some reason weren't allowed to go together. Poor Kevin was really upset and had to see a psychiatrist to help him mentally – no one seemed to realize we were really sad. I really missed my mum such a lot – she was more like a big sister, always playing with us. My foster mother was quite old and rather an unsmiling person, and she was often horrid to me, made me do lots of the housework and shopping for her so I didn't have time to do my homework properly. She had twin sons of her own, who were in trouble with the police and always fighting – I was scared of them.' On her sixteenth birthday, Katy was turned out of that home, 'so I ran to my boyfriend'.

By now, grown up beyond her years, Katy knew that the sole executor of her mother's will was her mother's bank manager. 'I knew he was renting our parents' house, which had no mortgage. I thought that now I was 16 I could live there with my friend and be able to look after Kevin. The manager said he'd think about it, but in fact he sold it for not much – it would be worth quite a lot today.' Katy, now married to her boyfriend, smiled. 'I think I'm quite wise now.'

According to Felicity Collier, chief executive of British Agencies for Adopting and Fostering (BAAF), up to 10,000 children are living with foster parents who are unknown or unchecked by Social Services. Private fostering is the least controlled and most open to abuse of all the environments in which children live away from home.

Serious as this situation is, there are hundreds of approved foster parents who are registered with their local authority and are wonderfully caring and trained people. As we heard in Chapter 2, they have sometimes begun their careers as responsible child minders. They often have children of their own, so the foster children, at any age from babies to 16-year-olds, come into ready-made families – most of whom are welcoming, well-adjusted youngsters, well used to a large and flexible family, unlike poor Katy's experience. However, the children of the foster parents must not be forgotten. Most are certainly well used to a house 'full of kids'. But the occasional child feels rather 'taken over' by an influx of strangers. Millie spoke with feeling: 'One time I felt that two of the boys were taking over my life – my parents, my brother, my toys. I knew they had unhappy homes, but that made me feel more guilty about resenting them.'

With the growing number of children in care, many more foster parents are needed across the country, even though they already provide homes for 65 per cent of all young people in care. One foster mother spoke from years of experience:

Most of the children who come into fostering are mentally

disturbed and we find that if these mental problems can be dealt with, then the inevitable learning difficulties that accompany them can more easily be overcome. Moving in and out of foster care is hard – social workers concentrate (quite rightly) on the children, but we find it difficult to have our opinions and suggestions listened to.

Another mother, who has fostered children for 15 years, says that 'It is a really rewarding thing to do. Yes, we are always busy, but when a child gives you a present on Mother's Day, and says he wants to share you with his own mother, it is a great feeling. Mind you,' she adds, 'it is difficult when the time comes for them to leave – often another big change for them and for me! But most of them keep in touch – some have come back to show me their own children!'

The reasons for a child living in foster care are numerous, and many are tragically far too familiar: as well as the death of parents, the rejection or abuse of children, the physical or mental disability of a birth parent, drug or alcohol problems in the family, or the break-up of many partnerships. The children concerned will inevitably have experienced far more than the average amount of change in their lives, and their families will have been constantly restructured. Some of the children themselves may have come from a term in the criminal justice young offending system. Being placed in foster care is yet another upheaval in their lives – often involving many changes and losses. They will experience separation from their parents, siblings and friends. It may well mean a move to a strange neighbourhood, a strange school. Even if they are relieved to be apart from violent or abusive relations, there will be deep feelings of loss, often of abandonment. Each child will react differently.

Susanna Cheal, Chief Executive of the Who Cares? Trust which works with children in care, says, 'Ninety-eight per cent of children come into care following family breakdown, not because of something *they* have done. They are often troubled, but not necessarily troublesome.' Many of the children come under the category of Special Needs. They may have severe learning disabilities, or suffer from emotional, behavioural or mental health problems. Some are also disabled physically. They will need tremendous understanding and emotional support both before and after any such moves. For all the adults concerned, this is a huge challenge, requiring many skills and resources, as well as real commitment. Telling a child what will be happening is a hard task, but once again you have to share as much truth – concrete information – as possible. 'Your dad has to go into hospital for a short while, and you know Mum can't cope on her own,' or 'This family have children your age and will be much easier to live with.' Always let the child know that *she* is not responsible for this new move. Of course, should her own behaviour be the cause, sometimes it is possible to suggest conditions for when she might return home again. Whatever the possibilities, professional counsellors advise that you remember a child will have different feelings from your own. She may not feel it is a 'happy' move, so it is unwise to promise that 'life will be better now'. What the child will need is to know she will be safe and with someone she can trust. She may be blaming herself for the latest move, feeling she has not measured up to her last carer's expectations in some way. Because of this, she may be reluctant to talk about her past, which she considers has been a failure.

How do you get such a child to relax and talk? Claudia Jewett, a leading US child and family therapist, has sound advice. She suggests that a good place to begin is to ask the child if there were any changes in the past that he has half-forgotten or is confused by. He will probably try to avoid dealing with any painful feelings connected with his past, but you should adopt a compassionate but firm attitude while continuing with your conversation. This you can do by suggesting that you take turns to provide information. 'Only ten minutes each, how about it?' The technique is useful – so you can get across the information you wish the child to hear, and he will often respond with all kinds of memories. These will help you discover just where the child needs most help. Obviously, both therapists and foster parents will have many ways of supporting a child through these difficult days – but they all stress that *listening* is still one of the best techniques if you want to obtain the confidence of a troubled child. Remember also that if you are talking with a very young child, she will need frequent updating on the reasons for her living arrangements, as her level of understanding grows.

There are an increasing number of excellent interactive books and worksheets for use among families, all of which can greatly assist in helping parents and others to communicate with and explore the feelings of the children in their care. Many of these are available from BAAF, from The Children's Society or from good bookshops (see Further Reading, p. 97).

One charitable organization which is changing the lives of many children – especially those in care or living in less than ideal family circumstances – is the Chance for Children Trust (see Sources of Help, p. 91). This was set up over a decade ago 'to help children and young people to grow emotionally, thus releasing their creativity so that they can express their feelings in a safe way'. They offer various therapeutic programmes with an emphasis on music and art, 'to build self-confidence and enable change and growth to take place'. Even very young children who have been emotionally damaged, or undergone long spells in hospital, are reacting wonderfully to the experience of music in their lives.

There will always be some children unable to find totally satisfactory foster placings (occasionally, children have been temporarily fostered with families practising a different faith to them); perhaps they never feel really wanted. The fact that they felt abandoned in the first place must weigh heavily on them all their lives. For them, another change will come when they leave care and are on their own, never having known a real home for long, and having missed out on so many of the things that are normal experiences for most children.

Facing adoption

The ultimate change in a child's life? Possibly. Foster parents are allowed, with Social Services' backing, to adopt a child who has been in their care for three years. Without such backing, they may legally adopt after five years. However, at least 75 per cent of foster parents do not adopt. Most child therapists agree that children may re-experience a sense of loss when a move as final as adoption cuts off any lingering hopes they may have had to be reunited with one or both of their birth parents. The most valid reason for adopting any child is, presumably, to protect that child – if, for example, a surviving birth parent is an abuser, violent, has disappeared, or is in prison.

It is vital to understand, for parents and children, that *adoption is for ever.* Of course, it could be comforting to a child who has been neglected or abused to be told that no one can ever take her away again, so long as she is loved and cared for. But it also means that the relationship between her and her natural parents is ended. A few of the foster parents who have decided to adopt a child, have pressed for continued contact with the birth family, but it seems to the majority of foster parents a wrong, not very happy, decision. The first three to four years after adoption are so fragile that such a step may well confuse a child – they have had enough change, and dread anything going wrong. On the other hand, an adoptive parent often tries *not* to talk to the children about the adoption, but care workers stress that this is also wrong. Children's feelings about their history, their parents and grandparents, can be powerful, and may increase as they grow older. Without any family to keep these feelings alive, this will be an ongoing loss.

4
Major Losses

A death in the family inevitably causes major changes. How can any parent or teacher prepare a child for such a tragedy? No prescribed lesson could possibly cover all the aspects and consequences of bereavement. But in homes where the subject of death is *not* taboo, where questions are answered truthfully, where a short illness or separation is clearly explained, the whole family are far better prepared for a serious loss.

It is not unusual for the first family death a child experiences to be that of a grandparent. The effect of such a loss will depend on how close the relationship has been.

If Grandfather or Grandmother has been a part of a child's life – perhaps lived in the family home or nearby – then it will be a bereavement they feel deeply. The two-generation gap may have created a very close relationship. Parents can be inclined to underestimate a child's grief (understandably, while mourning deeply themselves) but it must never be ignored. The questions, too, must always be answered. 'You said Granny was going to Heaven, so why did you bury her?' For a small child, the image of Granny's old dress or coat could be used. 'Granny's body was old, like her coat, no use to her any more – so it can be buried.' A happy follow-on would be for the child to be given something tangible of Granny's for a memento – perhaps a special brooch or a book they used to read together. Older children sometimes help to 'keep Gran's garden tidy', or 'We can feed Gran's cat now, she'd like that.'

Even when a grandparent has been a distant figure – perhaps living in another country – a child will learn something of the consequences of death from her parents' grief reaction. Don't hide your tears from the children. It is important for these to be seen and discussed, and for memories of the grandparent be kept alive with stories of their younger days and old photo albums.

Death of a parent

No loss can create so vast a disruption in a child's life as the loss of a

31

parent. The death of a mother or father will cause deep grief in any child, which must always be acknowledged. But if a child knows that the adults in her life are easy to talk with, and receptive to confidences and problems, this fact alone can be of the greatest comfort when a tragedy occurs. Although the Victorian days of lengthy periods of mourning have long gone, children, just as much as adults, need time to grieve. And it is during this sad time that children can be helped in their suffering without being over-whelmed, or even destroyed, by their emotions.

Above all else, children must be told the truth. They want to know how and why their father died, or how much their mother suffered. How you answer 'death' questions is *so* important to a child's conceptual development. Each child has individual needs and emotions. Many young children even suggest that they are in some way responsible for their parent's death. 'I didn't do what Mummy told me, and now she's gone!' Guilt is one of many emotions that they suffer, and as an adult, or perhaps a surviving parent, you have to reassure that child – time and again – that she was in no way to blame. 'Mummy loved you, always remember that.'

As time goes on, a child will want to know details of all the changes that are about to happen in his life. 'Who will make my sandwiches for school?' asked Lindy. 'How can I go to football on Saturday without Daddy?' was Ryan's sad question. Children are practical, and need practical answers. To quote Cruse – Bereavement Care: 'When someone in the family dies, the whole family changes in a way.' Even a baby will be aware of the sad feeling all around her. Although a parent's death does not necessarily mean that the family have to move house or that the children have to change schools, the whole atmosphere in a home will inevitably alter. Often children in the same family will have quite different reactions – one may want to talk, another may withdraw into himself.

When a mother dies

Following the death of a mother, there is a huge gap in the household – and although kindly aunts or friends may move in to help, nothing is quite the same. Each child will be feeling the loss in their own way – the youngest will yearn for Mum to put him to bed, the eldest will long for Mum to take her shopping. Meanwhile, Dad will be trying to cope with his own grief, and perhaps may not notice how much the children are suffering. Janey agreed. 'I was a teenager, and my dad sort of used me. He would take me to very unsuitable films, treating me like a partner, not a daughter. I don't mean he abused me – nothing like that. He had just adored my mother and missed her, so I felt it my duty to be with him and refused invitations to go out with my own friends.'

When Lindy's mother died, she and her two older sisters were told that their grandmother would come and live with them. The children had never met the rather solemn lady who arrived in time for the funeral. 'We didn't dare to ask her anything,' said ten-year-old Jessie. 'She gave us strange things to eat and made us get up too early in the morning, and wouldn't let Lindy stay up to watch TV with us. It was horrid – our lives were so different.'

It was a change in their lives that need not have caused quite such traumatic consequences, but their father was too deeply upset himself to notice how hard that poor grandmother was finding it to cope with three sad little girls.

Relationships between a father and his children when their mother has died can be complex as well as close. One little ten-year-old knows her father had to lose his wife for her to be born – thankfully a rare happening today. Her father adores her and has been a wonderful parent, but the little girl has always suffered feelings of guilt.

When another father lost his wife in childbirth, he was left with an 18-month-old daughter, Joanna. She did not have guilt feelings to contend with, but as she expressed it later she found herself 'mourning an absence'. At first her father tried to cope, but then he employed a series of housekeepers. Sadly, Joanna's first memory, around the age of four, was of being up to her neck in a bath of water, with the tap running. Her father came in and found the current housekeeper drunk, and saved the child. Needless to say, that housekeeper was sent packing. Joanna was then looked after by various relations – aunts and cousins. 'I was never in each of their homes for very long. Then one of the aunts wanted to adopt me, but my father refused. I was grateful for that. He was always very protective – visited me once a week.' When she was eight, her father remarried. 'He came to fetch me from my aunt, and on the way told me that my mother was waiting for me at home. This confused me – surely my mother was dead?' Once home, she met her stepmother, who insisted on being called Mum. 'She was never cruel to me, just indifferent. No mention was ever again made of my own mother, but at least I had a more normal life, no more changes of home or school.'

Field-Marshal Montgomery wrote in his autobiography of how he coped with his only son when his wife died. 'I could not bring myself to let my son see his mother suffering. He was only nine years old and was happy at school. After the funeral, I went to his school and told him myself. Perhaps I was wrong, but I did what I thought was right.'

It is easy, with hindsight, for all surviving parents to blame themselves for how they handled the tragedy – but psychiatrists all remind them that they did what they thought was right at the time. Try not to get bogged down with regret as well as your grief.

When a father dies

Samantha's father died when she was not quite three years old, and she remembers being told he was in Heaven. 'I pictured him lying on a cloud and thought I must get a very long ladder to reach him.' She was told few details of her father's death, and when only five was sent away to boarding school. 'I still feel there's a big gap in my life – a sense of something missing.'

Derek felt the sudden death of his father in a different way. 'I was a teenager and my friends began to call me Mr Spook, because I had no emotions – nothing ever fazed me. In situations where there is a lot of pressure I never break up. It has left me feeling that the actual death must not stimulate a change of behaviour for life. It is a child's reaction that counts – how he will cope with the rest of his life, not just with the death itself.'

Of course, the surviving parent, and other involved adults, *can* help a child to cope. Here again, honesty is essential. Many adults today will tell how, when they lost a parent in childhood, they were not told the truth. 'Daddy is away,' or 'Mummy is sick and can't come out of hospital.' Such horrendous stories were meant to protect a child, but of course only caused lifelong sadness and distress. It is no use pretending that lives will not change – often relationships within a family will alter drastically. Because of all these inevitable changes it is wise – if at all possible – to make sure that other more drastic moves should be avoided for at least six months. Moving house and schools can feel like a second bereavement to a grieving child.

When a mother loses her husband, the father of her children, her lover, possibly the major breadwinner of the family, her world is turned upside down. She may cry openly with her children, and this is good – shared grief is often therapeutic – but she will find it hard to keep the home running as it did before. Other mothers have been known to become afraid of dying themselves, or of losing other members of the family, and this unspoken fear often creates a claustrophobic atmosphere in the home.

'For me and my sisters it was terrifying,' recalls Sheila. 'Mum became so over-protective, we were stifled – she wouldn't even let us walk to school on our own!'

It is often thought that because a child does not express grief in the same way as an adult, he is not grieving. This may be because many children do not seem to suffer as much from the death itself as from its consequences and from the way it is handled by the surviving parent and others caring for the children. Certainly, the emotional reactions of the surviving parent can affect the children deeply – they may cause long-term social problems. All of which proves that children need to be given adequate, truthful information. Often the only experience a child has had of death is what he has seen on television – a violent, painful happening. Child psychiatrists suggest that allowing a child to see the body, to attend the funeral, to see how peaceful death can be, is so much better than leaving it all to a child's vivid imagination. Their fantasies are sometimes horrific!

Children's thoughts and feelings can be surprising in other ways, too, and totally unexpected by their parents. Some years after James' father died, his mother decided to marry again. She gave him and his sisters warning, and hoped they would understand how she felt. 'It's probably come as a bit of a surprise to you,' she said, although they had met their future stepfather many times. 'It certainly has to me – I never thought of marrying anyone else – never gave it a thought until now!' Then to her astonishment, James said, 'But it's one of the first things I thought of when Dad died!'

As we see time and again, children are very practical. James had known at once, even in the midst of his grief, that their lives were going to change for ever. Many of his friends had stepparents – mostly the result of divorce – and so he assumed his mother would remarry. None of us know exactly what goes on in our children's minds, so helping them to cope with any traumas is not an easy task for a surviving parent.

Helping a bereaved child

If a parent dies when young, it is usually due to an accident, or sudden illness – there is no warning of tragedy. How can anyone, let alone a child, absorb news that someone they loved, played and laughed with only hours before, is now *not alive*? Shock and then despair will follow. 'We had no time to say goodbye!' is so often heard amid the crying. No wonder adults try to hide the truth from their children, or at least postpone breaking the news. 'Anything to protect them.' But an experienced counsellor said, 'Children *can* cope with tragedy, face up to responsibilities, if they know the truth. And it is essential that their own strength is backed up by the support of a loving family.'

Of course, the drawn-out agony of terminal illness is no easier to bear than the trauma of sudden, perhaps violent, death. Again, counsellors' advice is to be honest. 'The illness must be acknowledged, and the nursing of it shared by the patient's family – the preparation for dying and bereavement can be a gradual process.' (See 'Hospice Care' in Chapter 7, p. 70.)

As well as fantasizing, children will suffer many of what the counsellors call 'bereavement reactions'. It can be frightening to be told that your child may suffer from shock, anger, denial, guilt, anxiety and despair. But whatever unusual, sometimes bizarre, symptoms of behaviour they display, try to accept these as normal. The child is as shocked as you are by the death, and must be helped through these bewildering emotions. It helps children, during the early days of bereavement, to know there are no right or wrong feelings. *How* you feel is what matters, and you must never be afraid to express what you feel. It is useless to ask a child, 'How are you feeling?' The answer will probably be 'Fine!' If you can express how *you* feel, and perhaps add, 'Do you feel like that sometimes?' you may get a far more honest response.

As the weeks go by, children may develop minor ailments – sore throats, aching limbs – especially if their parent died of an illness. Young ones may start wetting the bed, stammering, or become lethargic, overtired yet unable to sleep. There are no specific ways of helping each individual problem, but if you appreciate that each one is caused by a deep sorrow and a need for love and attention, then you will probably find practical solutions as you go along. Get the older children to teach the younger ones to kick a ball, cook biscuits or ride a bike. If one or other of them want to stay alone in their room, let them have their space – that is their way of coping.

On a practical level, try to keep the family's routine as unchanged as possible. If Mum always put their school clothes out each night, be sure these are arranged as before; if Dad provided pocket money on Saturday mornings, see it's continued. Although it is wise to acknowledge that life *is* going to be different from now on, the more old routines are kept up, the more secure the children will feel.

Talking about the person who has died is also helpful in most families – it is sad how many children are denied the comfort of hearing stories of their mum when she was young, and about their dad's love of cars or climbing.

'Mum kept talking about Dad after he died. She went on and on, and even told us about how they made love!' Sally, a teenager when her father died, recalled her mother's reaction with great understanding. 'I was upset at the time, and wished she would stop talking, but now I realize what a help it was. We all discussed Dad and the things he did – it was great. I'd hate to have missed that – it helped us all so much.'

But what about a child who seems to be stuck in her grief – whose behaviour really does seem uncontrolled, who shows intense vulnerability even to small separations, or shows signs of severe insomnia or suffers hallucinations? When should a parent seek professional help? A psychiatrist advises: 'Watch for grief that is delayed, prolonged or strangely disturbed. And take equally seriously grief that is absent.'

If you are worried, first speak with your family doctor. You may then be referred to a child guidance clinic, which will decide if your child is needing psychiatric help. Other parents have found great comfort in joining a widows' or other bereavement counselling organization, who can introduce you to specialists they have found helpful. There are also family groups, where talking with others in similar circumstances can be reassuring (see Sources of Help, p. 91).

Loss of a sibling

When a child loses a brother or sister, someone with whom he has shared so much of his life, a great wound is left. A young sister he teased and yet protected from older children at school has been killed by a car; an older brother he fought and argued with daily, but who was still his best friend and shared his bedroom, went to hospital and isn't ever coming home.

Quite apart from the deep sorrow, the changes in such a family are enormous. Tim, when his only brother died, was desolate. 'Now I'm an only child!' For Scott, the death of his sister meant that he was now the eldest in the family. And for many, many children, the death of a sibling means the relationships within their families undergo a huge change. There is often rivalry for their parents' love – and those parents may be so wrapped up in their own grief that they even forget they have other children.

More tragedy often follows, when Mother's and Father's grieving takes very different paths – paths that can never meet – and the family is torn apart rather than brought together by its sorrow.

Sadly, a child's death often follows a prolonged illness. Paul was nine when his sister died, aged seven. 'I used to lie in bed and cry and ask God not to let her die. Then when she did, it shattered my religion. For a long time I didn't believe she was dead (although I had seen her) and I remember sitting in that room with her. I think that when a child dies in a family it can be a make-or-break point for that family. I know that Mum and Dad had a very difficult time afterwards with my young brother and me – we still carry emotional scars.'

All the studies carried out by experts in child psychology emphasize how often the surviving children, following the death of a sibling, suffer from significant loss of self-esteem. There seems to be 'considerable idealization of the dead sibling, who was not only perceived by the child as more favourable than *self as I am*, but in many cases the child's own ideal. Thus for many children measuring up to the dead sibling seemed to be an impossible task.'

This is understandable when you consider what the death of a child means to parents. If it is a sudden death, the shock and despair can make them oblivious even to the presence of their other children. If it is a lingering illness, the attention lavished on the sick child is such that the siblings feel excluded, and even 'of little worth'.

'My parents talk about my sister as if she was some sort of saint. She certainly wasn't – she often told tales about me – but no one listened to me.'

No one listened to me. How often do you hear a child saying just that? I feel that this is when other family members, aunts, grandparents or close friends could – and should – step in and talk with those children.

When my friend died

When Polly died of leukaemia, it was the saddest day of her young life for her best friend, 12-year-old Julie. As her mother said, 'The two girls were inseparable. It was like losing a sister. Julie is quite lost.'

Losing a friend is not often thought to be such a traumatic event as losing a family member, but it can be equally tragic. 'When my friend died I sort of died inside too,' said Julie, now 19. 'I couldn't picture a future without her, couldn't talk with anyone else, felt that no one else understood me. It was the loneliest thing and on top of my own grief, I felt overwhelmingly sad for Polly. She didn't want to die, she loved life. She loved me too, as well as her family.'

Such a death may not involve any obvious changes to a friend's life – no moving house or school, no change of career, no lifestyle upheaval. 'But my life changed drastically,' said Julie. 'I had no one to walk to school with, to chat on the phone with, to do homework with, to spend weekends with, even to quarrel with as we sometimes did!' Polly's family were naturally deep in their own grief, and Julie felt rather left out. 'My mum and dad were kind, and Mum came with me to the funeral, but it was my teacher who listened to me most of all when I sort of freaked out one day at school. She understood how different my life was without Polly, and even introduced me to the school counsellor, who had a sort of quiet room where anyone could go who threw a wobbly at any time. For a long while I was scared to make any close friendships, and I still feel a gap in my life after all these years, but I reckon having someone to talk to at the time probably saved me from doing something stupid.'

5

Domestic Upheavals

Separation and divorce

Because divorce is commonplace today, it is sometimes assumed that the effect on children will be minimal, short-lived. Even with enormous family support, the opposite can be true. Apart from the drama of watching her parents splitting up, a child may lose one parent; have to leave her home, school and friends; have to divide her time between two homes; perhaps be divided from siblings; maybe lose contact with beloved grandparents. The disruptions to her home life will be as great as, sometimes greater than, those following a bereavement, and can affect her for many years.

There are two ongoing issues concerning divorce over which many experts have opposing views. The first is the controversy as to whether growing up within an *un*happy marriage is more damaging than the experience of separation. Some vehemently believe the opposite to be true. But what happens when children are brought into the discussion? Even in homes where bitter verbal or physical fighting is taking place, almost all say their lives would have been happier if their parents had not divorced. Nine-year-old Evan, whose parents yelled at each other night after night, was astonished and upset when they separated. 'A home isn't a family without a mum and a dad, is it?'

Conversely Nicholas, now a teenager, said: 'If only Dad had left years ago, we would all have relaxed. Mum used to try to overdose, she was so afraid of him. Now she's a different person.'

The other issue on which the professionals as well as the families concerned are still divided is to what extent, and for how long into the future, children are affected by divorce. There are those, such as the American professor and author Judith Wallerstein, who believe that divorce can 'cause deep damage to children, often rendering them incapable of forming proper relationships as adults'. Many others, whether from personal experience or academic research, report that parental separation causes little long-term damage. Of course, it is the type of loss and the handling of the family circumstances that matter.

Every family is unique. But for those who do go through divorce, the ensuing changes in their lives sometimes seem never-ending.

As with other major upheavals, children must be told what is happening or about to happen. Of course, whatever age they may be at the time, children will sense when their parents are not happy – when the arguments are becoming more serious, even violent, and the absences of either Dad or Mum become more frequent. But unless they are specifically told, they will try to put the idea of one parent leaving for good out of their minds.

Helen's parents had been living apart for several years. Then one day they took her out to lunch. 'They put on a show of friendliness and told me they were getting divorced. I was only eight and this was such a shock I cried – I was very upset – but my mother seemed surprised by my reaction. I remember feeling sort of unreal, in a dream. I remember voices physically over my head, which I suppose they were, shouting and arguing loudly.'

For Emily, only six at the time, her parents' arguments were part of her life. But she was shocked and upset when her father left home. 'I loved him and thought he loved me – I was terribly upset. Years later my mother told me about how violent he had been at times and I was appalled and asked her why she had never told me before. She said it was because she knew I thought him to be so great and probably wouldn't have believed her.'

Don also was not told why his parents had split up, or that it was to be a permanent arrangement. 'Suddenly Dad had gone. He never said goodbye, Mum just told me I could see him on Sundays. My whole life changed from that day on. Every Sunday morning I used to sit in the car with a kind of pounding in my head, and of course wanting to go there, yet afraid to see him – would he still be my dad?' In fact, Don's father was living with another woman who had two children of her own. 'There were this lady's kids all over the house, and it was like Dad was a stranger. He kept telling me how good they were, how clever, and I thought that he didn't want me any more. Yet Mum kept taking me there each week. How can parents be so insensitive?'

For many children, their parent's infidelity comes as a shock – a bitter pill to swallow. 'At first I was angry with my father, then angry with his girlfriend. And when my mother collapsed and needed comforting, my childhood seemed to end abruptly.'

This takes place in any family, a moment of growing up that happens when a child realizes his parents are not infallible and have weaknesses like any other humans. But in a divorce situation it can happen at an early age and can come as a sudden shock to a small child.

Most parents do try to consider the children, and bend over backwards to make the separation as smooth as possible. 'We told them what we had decided to do, that I would be moving to a new house in the next town, and that my husband would be staying here. We never argued in front of them, we let them stay with Granny and Grandpa while the move took place. I don't think they suffered nearly as much as I did.' Joy and Brian's mother really believed they were unfazed by their parents' decision, but the children, both young teenagers, had a different story to tell.

'We loved both our parents and knew they were trying to help us, but we felt we had no power whatsoever to arrange our own lives – they had been disrupted and we had no say at all in any of it. They just told us, never discussed it with us.' Those children never really settled into their mother's new home, which meant leaving their old friends and, worst of all, going to a new school – just before Joy's important exam year. But they were luckier than some, for their parents always kept in touch with each other, spoke on the phone, discussed the children's health and school activities. 'They never had to resort to talking through lawyers, which I guess was a crucial factor in keeping us all from getting too depressed.'

Milly was 14 when her parents divorced and her mother said, 'I'd like you not to tell anybody.' Perhaps her mother felt some sort of shame, remembering how ashamed *she* had felt when *her* parents had separated thirty years before – when divorce was comparatively rare. So poor Milly carried on this absurd attempt to keep her secret for some years, finally telling her best friend. 'I thought it strange you stopped inviting me around,' said the friend, who realized what a terrible pressure poor Milly had been under.

All her friends knew when Rosie's parents divorced, and one of them said, 'Your parents are divorced, so your dad is not really your dad any more!' Poor Rosie. 'That went through me like a knife,' she said. 'I felt he was being taken away by the sheer statement. She was only an ignorant child, but she was my friend and it meant a lot to me.'

It is one of the most important things that parents have to tell their children. 'Although we are divorced, and we are not husband and wife any more, we are still your mother and father – and always will be.' However drastically their lives will alter, that is one fact they must hang on to. As Scott, 15, said: 'Parents are parents for life, whether they are absent, or dead, or have run away, or are just uninterested in you – they are your parents for ever.'

Jo was 11, and his parents felt they were acting correctly. 'We must not treat him like a child,' they thought, and when they separated they asked their son to make the decision who he wanted to live with. 'It was like having to choose a person to be on your side in a game, when you know you could so easily hurt someone. I just asked them to stay together!' Now in his early twenties, Jo looks back at that time with a mixture of sadness and anger. 'It is too difficult a decision for a child – too much of a responsibility. On the whole, children like decisions made for them, they like a structure, some rules laid down. It gives them a feeling that someone cares and that there is some security and routine in their life.'

Wise words. We've already seen how important it is to prepare children before the divorce takes place; it is also essential to discuss the changes that will take place afterwards. For it is their normal routine that children miss when their home is divided. Not going to the same school, the same shops, the same playground. Who is going to take me to the sports centre on Saturdays? Can I still visit Grandpa? Can we take the cats and the hamster to the new house? And most worrying of all: 'Now Dad has left, will Mum leave me too one day?' Such anxieties abound, and with so many changes happening in their lives, all the questions need to be answered, all the new arrangements fully explained, and constant reassurances given that they will never be abandoned.

When a family breaks down because of clashes of religions or cultures, the children's anxieties can be doubled. Donna's husband was a Muslim, and when they married she had converted to his faith and agreed that their two children could also embrace his beliefs. However, after nine years Donna decided to revert to her own Anglican church, and this caused her husband to leave her. Imagine the problems those children faced – loving both their parents, both their cultures. Donna was awarded custody of the children, although her husband went on living nearby. She was afraid he might take them with him to his own country, and so would accompany them each time they visited him. They hated this, for they loved their father. The change in their relationship with each parent was as hard for them as the divorce.

Violent marriages that lead to divorce

When parents separate for more traumatic reasons, the changes children have to face are never easily explained. Cynthia was happily married with three children. When they were nine, seven and only two years old, her husband began to be violently abusive towards her. She would try never to let the children hear their quarrels, but of course they could see her injuries, and at times she would end up in Casualty and their grandmother would have to come in to help. 'I was determined not to upset their routine,' their mother said. 'Even if we had all had a noisy night, with little sleep, I sent them to school each day. I explained to their teachers why they might fall asleep at their desks, and they let them do just that.' Cynthia felt that sometimes the teachers would treat the children in a special way, which was understandably kind, but she never wanted them to feel in any way 'different'.

Two days before her husband finally left her, he and Cynthia had a noisy disagreement over something one of their sons had been doing. Afterwards, the poor boy felt that his father had gone because of him. 'It's all my fault,' he insisted. This is such a familiar cry for children who have lost a parent. Cynthia realized this, and kept repeating to all her children that they were in no way to blame for the divorce. She has other advice to give to parents in her position: 'When friends tell you that children are resilient and will soon get over it, don't believe them. They are not nearly so resilient as adults believe. Yes, at first they do seem unaffected, but it can take time – weeks, months, even years – before they have any serious reactions. It was two years before my eldest son's school work began to suffer. I know that in time any one of them may need counselling.'

Cynthia obviously agreed with Judith Wallerstein on this subject, and in order to help her children cope she also learned that she has to be honest with them all the time. 'Always tell them the truth. My children actually told me they *wanted* the full truth – and that was several years after we had divorced.'

Because children need to hear the truth, they also need to talk themselves. Often, they find it hard to talk to either of their parents – whether they live with them or not. This is natural, and it is a wise mum or dad who understands this and is not hurt when a child will pour his heart out to others and not to them. 'My child has a list of numbers on his mobile phone, friends of mine and of his, all of whom he can ring and have heart-to-heart talks with.' This is an excellent idea. Also, if a child meets up with others in his peer group who are in the same position, it will be of great help to him. There are several organizations throughout the country where parents and children can meet and talk, such as Gingerbread. This is a well-known group where single parents and their children can get to know each other, go for outings and picnics together, and hear how other families are coping (see Sources of Help, p. 91).

Contact centres

When a father's violence is extreme or a mother is seriously mentally disturbed, so that any contact at all seems a threatening situation, a court welfare officer can arrange visits within a pre-arranged place (in some areas this is called a Saturday Centre). For parents who wish never to meet, it is often the only way to arrange contact. The parent with whom the children are living can take them to the Centre and hand them to the officer, who will accompany them to a room where the other parent is waiting. The 'other' parent may well feel this is like a prison visit, but it would be sad for the children and both parents if such an arrangement was turned down. Playing with a small child, talking with an older one, possibly just reading or playing cards together, will keep up the all-important contact. In time, things may change – and once trust is built up it may be possible for freer visiting.

For Jennifer, aged nine, who lived with her mother, the first visit was scary.

I hadn't seen my dad for nearly a year and I missed him, though Mum wouldn't talk about him so I just had to keep his face in my mind. When we got to the Centre, a lady came and asked Mum if she wanted to come in with me, but she said she didn't want ever to see 'that horrible man' again. So I went on my own with the lady who took me to a room where my dad was sitting by himself. The lady said we could play a game of cards, or snakes and ladders, and Dad asked me what I wanted to do. I really wanted to go for a walk with him like when I was little, but we played games on a table and he asked me if Mum was all right. I said she was fine, and when it was time to go I kissed Dad goodbye and he didn't hug me like he used to. He looked so sad I wanted to cry. Mum wouldn't listen when I talked about Dad and what we had played together, so I never told her that he had asked after her. Visits after that were not scary at all, and I used to take books in to read, and show him drawings that I had done at school. I really looked forward to the visits.

Living in a refuge

Pip and Tricia's mother never talked about their father's violence, although they had lived with it for most of their young lives. But it came as a shock – an unforeseen change – when she suddenly took them away with her to a women's refuge. This involved huge losses for them, not only of their home, but of their school and friends – all left behind after their hurried departure one night. 'I had to leave my cat behind, too,' said Tricia. But this was just their first move. Several more times they had to travel, sometimes miles away, to a different refuge, a different school, only to be dragged off again before they had time to settle in. They could not fully understand the reasons for living like that – they knew their mother was afraid of their father beating her up, but he had never been cruel to them and they missed him. After about a year they went home again, and it wasn't until they were back at their old school that their mother told them their dad was in prison. Now a new routine took place in the family – yet another change! They have only been able to visit the prison once. 'It was good to see Dad, and we liked going as it was near the seaside and we were allowed to go on the beach.'

Stepfamilies

One of the main reasons for divorce is when father or mother, or both, find new partners. A dramatic change for all the children involved. Suddenly the word 'stepfamily' echoes around. And it must be remembered that all stepfamilies are born from loss – through death, divorce or separation. As we know, loss can cause endless upheavals in a family, and when a child suddenly finds himself with two or even three families instead of one, it is bewildering and may have disastrous consequences. Don voiced what many children feel when they are first introduced into a new family. 'How would our parents feel if suddenly we said you are going to have a new husband or wife, not of your choice? Yet they say calmly to us – or don't even tell us, it just happens – that we are given a new mother or father!'

I hope that most parents today do not let this vast change in a child's life 'just happen'. 'My parents got divorced when I was nine, and my mum married someone else straight away. I didn't know what was happening, and I didn't know where my other dad went to. And now I see my mum and my stepdad much more than I see my dad, which I think is quite unjust.'

And remember little Joanna, who had no warning of a stepmother's arrival and then had to call this strange lady 'Mum'.

Stepparents should never expect, or ask, to be thought of as 'Mother' or 'Father'. Once again, birth parents have to talk openly with the children, and reassure them of their determination to create new, happy homes. If your children feel they can always come to you and talk out their worries, many previously unspoken fears and fantasies can be allayed. For there are many fantasies about stepparents – the wicked stepmother, the abusive stepfather. Sadly, some are not just fantasy. However, many children do find that the 'new' family set-up is a happy one, far happier than their original home. 'I had never seen real affection before – togetherness, I suppose you call it – my mum and Chris (he never wanted us to call him Dad, thank goodness) laughing and sitting in a warm, cosy kitchen. It was marvellous.'

Other children are constantly in a state of transition, their lives rarely free from disruption and acrimony. A child who has always lived with a single mum is plunged into a large family; a girl whose mother has died has to live with her father who has remarried and now has two other children she has never met before; another boy whose mother has been divorced twice is traumatized by the thought of yet another stepfamily. It is vital for all these children to be

47

reassured that they are still loved. It is what all children want and need – to be loved and also understood. They need plenty of time to prepare for all these changes in their lives – to be told all the details of what is happening. 'Will I still be able to visit Dad or Mum?' is often a burning question – and children need time to consider all the new arrangements.

Most significantly, they will need plenty of warning if they are to meet stepbrothers and sisters. Pete had been an only child, and was suddenly confronted with a brother and sister. 'For a long time I felt it was so unfair – they had each other to grumble with, I didn't.' Joan, who had been the eldest in her family of three girls, suddenly found herself with two more older sisters. 'I was bossed around and I resented it.'

Sometimes the stepchildren of all the families involved get to become friends. 'We sort of banded together, all seven of us,' said Janey. 'Our parents would be shouting their heads off yet again, and we would disappear into the garden and have a kind of conference. One time the two youngest suggested we all run away, and the two eldest agreed, but as it was nearly a hundred miles to our old home we said we'd stay! I suppose it was a sort of search for a way to take the reins – we all felt we had no power whatsoever to arrange our lives which had been so disrupted.'

Certainly, I have met many families whose assorted children have become good friends, and then when a 'joint' baby appears, and they all become labelled as 'Yours, Mine and Ours', they settle down amazingly well.

For Craig, the word 'stepparent' has many connotations. 'Well, there's Penny who lives with my dad, but before her there was Kathy and before her was Rachel. And Mum is living with James, but says she might marry Peter.' In many a classroom today his story is not unusual. But whatever the circumstances, new families mean huge changes – each set of parents will have different lifestyles. Within some households, small differences such as strange mealtimes or varied routines for bedtime and weekend activities will be difficult at first. In some 'new' families, children will be bewildered by disciplines and rules that can be frightening. 'We were never allowed to watch TV during the week, and my stepdad wouldn't let Mum take me to school – he said I was old enough at seven to go on my own.'

48

This is one area where the birth parent the child lives with could prepare her children for the changes there will be in a new household. She can remind them that all families plan their lives slightly differently, and explain that there is no right or wrong way to do things. 'Mum told us that in our stepdad's house no dogs or cats were allowed on the beds, but in her house it would be all right.'

Other stepparents ignore the children completely. 'My stepmother wasn't unkind, she never hit me or anything, but she never loved me, either – just cooked the meals and checked I was in the house at bedtime – that's all.'

For Steven and Brett, their stepfather seemed 'a nice man'. Their own father, who had been horrifically violent towards their mother, was living in the next town, and they would visit him once a fortnight. He would tell them that their stepfather was horrid, cruel, and that on no account were they to tell him they liked him. They were not even allowed to mention his name. The boys knew that if they disobeyed their father, he would hit them. Steve, at ten, would just lie to his father, then go home and tell his stepfather how much he liked him. Brett, only five, was not so good at lying! 'Dad told me I didn't like you,' he said to his stepfather, 'but I think I do!'

Molly also never looked forward to visiting her father, who had walked out on his family without even saying goodbye. 'I don't want to go and see Dad really, but I do go because he buys me things!'

One experienced stepfather summed up the many changes that children have to face in all these circumstances: 'They are presented with divorce, a move of home, changing friends, the loss of a parent; rows and tensions are dumped on them; they have had a massive upheaval and people thrust on them without their wanting any of it.' And he added, 'I admire those children who come through it unscathed. Perhaps as adults we have not even begun to understand what we've put on these children.'

Wayne, who bravely talked of his family consisting of 'more steps than the Eiffel Tower!' became remarkably philosophical during his teenage years. 'The emotional reality is that when their parents split up, children do suffer guilt, rage, grief and even relief, frequently all at once,' he remarked. 'Even so, they can, and do – with the respect and love of those around them – become happier again.'

6

The Adolescent Years

There comes a time when the children themselves are the cause of changes in family life. That time is adolescence. Your little girl or boy is suddenly – yes, it seems to happen overnight – a teenager.

So what is adolescence? We all know it is the period in human development that occurs between the beginning of puberty and the onset of adulthood. But what is puberty? Doctors tell us it is the period at the beginning of adolescence when the sex glands become functional. And we all know what that means: our teenagers undergo enormous physical changes, when raging hormones begin to kick in and confused emotions overtake childhood dreams. As a child psychologist wrote, 'It would be abnormal if they were not confused at times – even scared.'

Pauline was one of many mothers who realized that she had never discussed puberty with her daughters. 'My own mother never told me anything – starting my periods came as a shock to me – but I managed with the help of friends. So when my daughters said they had sex education at school, I was quietly relieved, and thought there was no need for me to tell them anything else.'

But her children were typical of so many. They had biology lessons, sex lessons, and thought they knew it all. But there is more to growing than being able to name the body parts on a diagram. To quote from the *American Family Physician* of July 1999: 'The way children see their own body has a lot to do with their self-esteem. It is important to let children know they are OK the way they are and that you love them that way.' Wise words. For if you start talking with your children *before* the onset of puberty about the changes that will take place, they will far more readily accept that they are OK, that whatever changes they may experience are natural. Try to do this without making it a big deal, and answer their questions as clearly as possible. And this means starting to talk when they are still in primary school, for some girls actually start puberty as young as eight years old – the average age being around 11 – and boys around 12.

For girls, we automatically think to warn them of their first period. Do explain this loss of blood in plain language – there are adults today who were never given a truthful explanation and for whom it all came as a complete surprise! Maggie says that only forty years ago, when she was ten, she had never been told anything. 'When I saw what was happening to me I thought I was really ill. I was almost too frightened to tell my mother, as I knew how upset she'd be if I died! We'd had no sex education at school, biology lessons were all about frogs, not humans! Mind you, even then my mother didn't really explain very well – she told me it meant I would be able to have babies. That seemed a bit daft to a ten-year-old, and having no sisters I had to resort to reading books in the library.' Hopefully, mothers today give better guidance to daughters, but it's worth checking also that sisters or friends have discussed the subject, and the use of tampons and so on. Don't forget it is a big moment in a girl's life emotionally as well as physically – they may well have many practical anxieties. 'How will I know when it's going to start? Could it happen in front of the class?' 'Will other people always know when I'm menstruating?' Agony Aunts say they get endless queries such as this from girls, well before they reach their teens. Don't be upset if your daughter prefers to consult an outsider – show her you admire her independence and are always ready to listen if she needs more guidance.

Most mothers say that when they approach the subject of body changes – enlarged breasts, pubic and armpit hair, and so on – their daughters will say they know it all. 'My child laughed and said she probably knew more than I did!' And they may well have discussed these changes with their peers, or with older sisters, but there is probably still quite a lot they don't know. Just because they don't ask questions, it doesn't mean they know all the answers. Many of them worry if they develop earlier or later than their friends, and this confirms what many doctors and child therapists advise: let your children know that they are normal. There may be an average age for children's mental, emotional and physical growth, but the variations are most noticeable at adolescence. Your elder daughter may have her first menstrual period at ten, and your younger girl not until she is 16, and both are entirely normal. Of course, some of them feel afraid of growing up. Thirteen-year-old Gillian was in tears when she noticed herself developing, while another girl was really excited and told her mother, 'You can't boss me around any more now I'm an adult!'

It is not unusual for fathers to be dismissed when they approach their sons with advice. 'Thanks, Dad, I learned all that at school,' is a common answer. But at least it seems wise to let your children know that you care, that you are there if and when they do want advice. And many do. One 14-year-old boy was distraught because he still had a high voice, undeveloped reproductive organs and no body hair. 'My friend is the same age as me and he has a deep man's voice and adult genitalia and he has to shave nearly every day – what's wrong with me?'

For single parents, this time in their children's lives can be even more difficult. Mothers on their own with sons often resort to studying books on teenage problems, unless they are fortunate enough to have helpful brothers or uncles in the family. 'How on earth am I expected to discuss wet dreams with my 14-year-old or help him shave?' A familiar cry from a single mum! And a single father with two daughters said that he had to seek advice from all the female relations he could find. 'I could see the girls were changing, but felt helpless. We had been very close, but now they seemed a bit distant. It was sad.'

A first change, which teenagers hate and are often ashamed of, is when they get spots. All you can do, apart from the obvious cleanliness and diet suggestions, is to tell them that this is a phase, all part of their body changing. Explain that acne is caused by sweat glands, and is in no way their fault.

Sexual awareness

We're talking here about the obvious physical signs that appear – but when do all these sexual hormones start playing up? They can begin to be pretty active at around 14! Which, of course, is the reason your slap-happy schoolboy is turning into a rebellious young man, and your laughing schoolgirl into an unkempt and unsmiling young woman. They are confused – they want to be adults one moment and children the next – they are in turmoil. But so are you – so is your household!

Parents' comments on these changes in their children range from 'difficult', 'rebellious' and 'uncommunicative' to 'out of control'. Yet they all long to be able to help their youngsters to cope during these adolescent years. How? There are countless books, parenting courses, advisory centres, self-help groups and even videos, all of which give practical advice to worried mothers and fathers. In one short chapter I do not intend to add to the list! However, I have spoken with many parents and their teenagers who are happy for me to tell their stories. I hope that some of them may provide a little encouragement – if only by showing you that you are not alone, and that things *do* get better. As one mother said, 'When the hormones settle down, the children start to think more like adults – it's just hell going through it.'

What many parents forget is that it is hell for their teenagers as well as for them. The expression 'Troublesome Teens' has become a cliché, and all adolescents are assumed to be 'perpetrators of violence and crime, doing drugs or being prostitutes'. Adjectives such as 'wild', 'ruthless', 'moody' are directed towards them – especially from the media. On films and videos, in magazines and newspapers, they are seldom portrayed as anything other than 'wild joy-riders' or 'boorish thugs'.

One 20-year-old recalls his teen years: 'I remember feeling moody and irritable a lot of the time. I thought I was about to become violent or something. I didn't have a real reason to be stressed or anything, I have a great family. But I thought maybe I ought to try drugs – I was a teenager, wasn't I? Thanks to a super teacher at college I came through it all, but the odds seem to be against us.'

At times they seem to be against parents, too! This is understandable. When your 16-year-old becomes aggressive, over-confident and apparently unwilling to listen to any adult advice, you become filled with self-pity. How can I cope? You have to start by reminding yourself that your problem teenager is still a child and is also desperately in need of guidance. Once again, as all the professionals tell us, we must communicate with our children, respect them, and stop telling them what to do. Negotiate with them, they insist. Easier said than done!

Family guidelines

However, it is true that in families where talking has always been open and children always listened to, it won't be quite so hard to get through the adolescent years. Then when there are problems in the family you will all be used to talking about them – not avoiding them. Discussion with many parents and their teenagers (separately!), with teachers and child psychiatrists, reveals surprisingly similar guidelines they all offer to parents:

1 From the beginning, always lay down reasonable rules.
2 As parents, or stepparents, decide all rules together – always present a united front. (Teenagers sometimes drive a wedge between two parents if they suspect they are not in agreement.)
3 Let the teenagers know their boundaries.
4 When they disobey – which they will – you have control, because they knew the rules.
5 Understand that being a teenager today is different from when you were one.

Whatever they may say, teenagers like discipline – without it, they have nothing to rebel against. As one 17-year-old said, 'I don't agree with my parents' ideas, but I respect them.' It is surely good also if your teenage children know that you trust them. One mother said she was badly let down when her two daughters were not home by the time she had stipulated. 'I was angry, because I knew I was right to insist on a curfew. They had no excuse.' And by sticking to her rule, which she felt to be right, she was duly rewarded. The following week the girls were home in good time. 'So Mum gave us a treat.' 'Yes,' said their mum, 'they deserved it because they had played fair. I told them I can now trust them – it's all part of growing up.'

Advisers from the Tavistock Clinic in London agree that setting boundaries (just as you did with your toddlers) is essential. They also suggest that you listen to your teenagers' views and arguments *before* you begin to negotiate with them – do hear them out. Many angry sessions may follow – plenty of door-slamming may take place – but you have to put up with that!

Once you achieve a rapport with your children – however long that may take – then when the inevitable subjects of petting, sexual activities, birth control, sexual diseases, etc., arise, hopefully you will be able to discuss them freely together. Again, they may think they are street-wise, but many are just behaving in a know-it-all manner which is probably hiding a lack of self-confidence. 'I learned all about sex from films and television,' said Amanda, aged 16, 'but I knew nothing about relationships or what it was like to be a mother. My best friend got pregnant when she was 14, and the boy ran away. I dreaded having a baby myself, and finally I got my mother to talk with me.'

Telling youngsters not to have sex is not enough: they have to know why. 'Apart from the obvious risk of pregnancy, under-age sex is illegal,' says Amanda. 'But more than those reasons, Mum explained that you have to be emotionally ready, and I know I'm not! And when you think of all the physical dangers, like Aids – wow!'

Amanda is lucky. Her mother has steered her away from the pop group culture that promotes the belief that if you are not having an active sex life by the time you are 15, you are not 'with it'. One girl, on her fifteenth birthday, became seriously depressed. 'I'm not normal,' she cried. The media, too, sends out messages that make teenagers assume it is normal to have several sexual partners. This despite recent research by a consultant on adolescence which shows that: 'By 16 only one in five girls and one in four boys have actually had sexual intercourse.' Possibly a reassuring message for parents and their teenagers. Today they are not afraid to discuss sex openly, and are fully aware of what 'safe sex' means. But the constant pressure on youngsters to enter into full sexual relationships at far too early an age is not just wrong – it is sad. Apart from the fact that they all mature at different paces, how many teenagers are learning, like Amanda, that loving feelings *must* be in there?

The importance of relationships is something that is seldom discussed with boys. They may know all about the physical dangers and the methods of birth control, but when it comes to understanding their emotions and those of their girlfriends, that is often an unknown area. Boys are far less likely to discuss their problems with each other than girls. To help them, perhaps you could liken it to learning how to drive a car. It's not difficult to master the clutch, even to understand the workings of the engine, and to learn the Highway Code. But those are only the basics of actually driving on a public road. You have to respect the other drivers, think 'road courtesy' rather than 'road rage', and in the early years acknowledge that good, unselfish driving can only come with experience. A lesson well worth applying to relationships with the opposite sex.

Within single-sex families this is a hard lesson to teach or learn. Boys and girls, however many friendships they have with the opposite sex, seldom understand the different emotions they are both struggling with. 'My girlfriend changed so much in a few months I was fed up and told my mother about it. She was pretty cool, didn't laugh or anything, but she told me to think how much I had changed too.' That 15-year-old was fortunate in having a mother who realized he needed a first lesson in relationships.

The eminent US psychosexual therapist Dr Ruth Westheimer writes of three important things for teenagers to remember concerning sex: 'Don't ever feel that you have to do anything you don't want to do. Don't feel guilty about your thoughts or fantasies. Don't ever try to force someone else into doing anything he or she doesn't want to do.'

Among all the other confusions in their thoughts, teenagers often query their own sexual orientations. When such subjects are openly talked about today, it is hopefully one that is brought up in sex lessons and discussions. But it is understandable if doubts sometimes enter a young person's mind. 'Am I gay?' 'Do I really prefer women to men?'

One 15-year-old boy was sexually abused by his sports teacher. After his initial shock, and before he had any ideas about telling his story to friends, his first reaction was to wonder if *he* had attracted the man. 'Maybe I'm homosexual!' He was fortunate in having a father who noticed his son's unusual reluctance to talk about his sports teacher, and the boy told him what had happened. His father had the sense to reassure his son that it was the *teacher's* preference, not his, that led to him being the victim of such an attack. Another instance where the freedom to have open discussions within the family is a huge help in surviving the many teenage anxieties.

However openly you may have talked with your children over the years, you're probably feeling that you are having to struggle to cope with all the changes your teenager is inflicting on the family – life is so different in the twenty-first century. A huge worry for parents is their teenagers' use of the Internet – chat rooms and dating lines are temptingly available. So how on earth can you help your teenager without endless family arguments? The Home Office has produced a booklet for parents of 11- to 14-year-olds which offers help and advice about staying safe online. For copies, phone 0800 771234.

Meanwhile, just being available when needed is one way to help, and allowing them what they consider much-needed privacy is another. Try not to show *your* anxiety. Telling them you feel you have failed as parents will only add feelings of guilt to their other confused emotions. If they know that whatever they do or say you still love and care for them (remembering that love and hate are pretty close at times!) then you should all survive.

Serious changes to watch out for

But what if you notice changes other than those we all expect? Is your child changing his eating habits, losing interest in his usual hobbies or sport, excessively moody, or not bringing his friends home any more? When should you start to worry? Girls often try to change their appearance, wishing they were someone else. Before reaching their teens, they often turn to teenage magazines, reading articles on 'How to Become a Teenager', and then try to emulate the slim models by not eating. Yes, anorexia is all about lack of self-esteem and confidence, as is a sadly growing tendency among 13- to 15-year-olds, mostly girls, to self-harm. They cannot bear the pain of their mental problems, and find emotional and physical relief from them by cutting, burning or even self-strangulating themselves. Perhaps your quiet, compliant daughter, silently reading her maga zine, seems easier to deal with than her more rebellious brother. But, as counsellors tell us, self-harming youngsters like to keep their problems secret, so do keep communication lines open if you can.

A recent research project confirmed that this bizarre habit of self-affliction is almost entirely due to traumas suffered in childhood. In other words, it is the pain inside themselves that they are trying to get rid of. It is perhaps a wild hope that physical pain could relieve their emotional distress, overpower the mental agony. It is not an attempt at suicide. As one teenager explained, 'If I wanted to kill myself, I'd cut a vein, not just my skin.' Nor are all these young people seeking attention. 'There are less painful ways of doing that!' said one girl rather bitterly. In fact, most of the girls carefully hide their injuries, cover up their arms and legs, so that they are sometimes not detected.

Coping with a child who self-harms needs a trusted adult with listening skills rather than judgmental advice. Even doctors and nurses often dismiss the young people as 'time-wasters'. It may, as some teachers suggest, be a passing phase. But it is usually a sign of serious disturbance, perhaps within the family, and must be recognized, and professional help sought if necessary. As a parent, do try to keep your relationship going – talk together if you can, discuss the family problems. Just talking about them could relieve some of your youngster's pain. She will probably have deep-rooted worries. If these can be addressed, and the child helped to find healthier ways of dealing with them, the self-harm should no longer be necessary.

Drugs

The trick is to be concerned without causing alarm – easier said than done! You may well jump to the conclusion that they are trying drugs, although any slightly bizarre changes are often a natural sign of growing up. Doctors and teachers advise that the best way to deal with your suspicions is not to accuse a child outright: before you discuss drugs with him or her, decide what you want to say and the best way of getting your message across. Remember too, that your teenagers may well know more about drugs than you do, so do get well informed before starting a discussion. (See Sources of Help, p. 91.) Once you know the facts, doctors suggest that you:

1 Ask your child his views on drugs, and try to listen with respect to what he has to say.
2 If you suspect he is lying to you, try not to get angry, but explain that your concern is for his health and well-being.
3 Try not to threaten him with punishment – this might seem to offer a quick solution, but it's unlikely to give the results you are looking for.
4 Make sure he understands that he is responsible for his actions and the consequences that follow.

Meanwhile, it is important to remember that most young people who do try drugs do *not* continue using them. Most of them try them because their friends use them, or simply because they are curious about the effects. And, as we are now all aware, drugs are easily available.

Alcohol problems

Another growing problem among teenagers is alcohol. In some ways this is a more difficult problem to argue against than drug abuse, in that it is a socially acceptable activity. 'Well, you and Mum drink, don't you? I only had beer, where's the harm in that?' Many times, there will be no harm done at all – peer pressure as well as curiosity, trying to prove your adulthood, and sheer defiance, can tempt all youngsters to 'have a go' at cigarettes, alcohol and drugs. You can only warn them of the health dangers, the criminal penalties and the damage to themselves and their families in the future. Experienced educational counsellors advise that keeping teenagers fully occupied with other activities is a well-proven method of preventing them from becoming addicted to any of the many substances so readily on offer today. Football, hockey, running, will keep them healthy as well as busy – and sports centres that provide swimming, gymnastics, basketball and skating can help to keep them from spending time on street corners. Even a small success at a sport – swimming twenty lengths, or being picked for a basketball team – is often enough to recover a lost confidence, so they will have no need to look elsewhere for self-esteem.

Often, an addiction starts with a longing to be part of a peer group. A child may be lonely. She may well be looking for help – however street-wise she may appear. If she knows that you are always ready to listen and not criticize, you might just save her from turning to a bottle or a tablet.

These vital subjects cannot be discussed in half a chapter! But apart from speaking with your GP or your child's teacher, there are many helpful organizations to which you and/or your teenagers can turn for advice. (See Sources of Help, p. 91.)

There is ongoing controversy about the various methods of lecturing children on the drastic consequences of taking drugs or alcohol, of joy-riding, of theft and violence. In these days of television there is little our children have not seen or heard – but documentaries can so easily be confused with fiction. The police visit schools to talk about the effects of all such illegal behaviour. They give graphic descriptions and pull no punches. These more personalized warnings must surely prevent at least some schoolchildren from experimenting with illegal substances or becoming involved in street crime. Yet if these warnings are not discussed within the home as well as the school, they may be looked on as 'just another lecture'.

Anne and Robert were thought of as exemplary parents, always taking huge interest in their two sons' and one daughter's activities – academic and sporting. 'Our middle son never gave us a day's worry until he was 15. With no warning, his whole mental attitude changed. We accepted it as the inevitable teenage turmoil, told him we understood and so on. But he never smiled from that day on – and to our dismay he was twice brought home by the police after a disco brawl. Even then, we felt he would grow out of it. But we didn't ignore it – we sought advice from our doctor, from his school, from family advice groups, and from our church. Maybe we tried too hard?'

Poor Anne, she and her husband suffered for so long, yet they always remembered to help their other two children to survive the criticisms and taunts of some of their schoolmates. 'Your brother's a junky!' they would jeer. Their brother did eventually become a heroin addict – a sad story, which his parents wanted told 'so that other mothers and fathers would be helped to understand that it is not always their fault when their children stray'. Their daughter added her comment: 'Our lives were never the same again, and it broke Mum's and Dad's hearts – and yet they still didn't forget about our grief at losing our brother. They helped us all to get through it together.'

Such stories remind us how hard it is to know when adolescent angst turns to depression. Specialist psychologists in adolescent problems remind us that we all have strong emotions – and that if we can get our teenagers to understand that all their emotions, all their feelings, are what life is about, we can prevent serious depression taking hold. After all, what they are doing is searching desperately for an identity. As a parent you must never take it personally, but your children want to discover that they are not just your son or daughter, but themselves.

Separating parents sometimes forget their teenagers

Among all these worries during the teenage years, there are many lesser events that cause significant changes in an adolescent's life, which are often completely unnoticed by their parents.

In the previous chapter we saw how divorce can affect young children, but it is often forgotten that children in their late teens – possibly setting off for college, or starting work, even setting up home with a partner – may feel equally upset. 'Suddenly I felt as if all support from home had gone. I was angry and confused, even though I was excited at going to university.' Certainly it was not a good time for Keith's parents to divorce. They may have felt that having waited until their children were striking out on their own was sensible timing, but they had forgotten how much they were still needed.

One 19-year-old girl explained her feelings when she was starting in her first job: 'I had just settled into my flat when Mum told me she was leaving Dad. I knew she was happy in a new life, and I was glad for her, but I knew Dad was lonely and needed my support. Then my granny took my mum's side, and I suddenly began to realize that if I had children myself, they wouldn't have a happy set of grandparents to visit like I had. Perhaps I was selfish, but going home wasn't ever the same again. I mean, which one of them *was* home now?'

An afterthought baby

Another time when parents tend to ignore their teenager's feelings, or perhaps misinterpret them, is when Mother unexpectedly becomes pregnant. 'An afterthought, but what fun it will be!' announced one mum to her 14-year-old daughter and 15-year-old son. Their shocked faces should have told her that 'fun' was not the word they would have used. For in spite of all the sexual knowledge we understand our children have learned from an early age, and no matter how wisely we have discussed such matters with them, they can be extremely prudish at the idea of their parents 'still' having sex. 'It can be oddly disturbing, just at a time when a teenager is discovering his own sexual feelings,' say many experts on adolescent matters. 'Some find it all rather a joke, others find they are jealous.'

'This is one change we could do without,' said Lawrence, aged 15. 'The house seems full of baby junk, and Dad is walking around pretending to be a young father again – it's embarrassing.' The way the arrival of a new baby is greeted will finally depend on the family dynamic – if they have all been loved and loving among themselves, then the older children will never feel displaced or neglected. Girls, particularly, will usually take on a motherly role to a tiny baby, and boys too can learn to enjoy being a role model for a much younger brother or sister.

'But do remember to give them extra attention – just as you would if they were little again,' said Sue after her baby was born. 'I take my sons out on their own whenever I can, to show them how special they are.'

Teenage pregnancy

There is another, more disturbing reaction to this open announcement of sexual activity between their parents. Teenagers in the throes of finding their own sexual identity can be tempted to practise one-upmanship and become sexually competitive.

However, this is seldom the direct cause of teenage pregnancy. For in spite of all the warnings, more than 8,000 girls under 16 get pregnant in Britain every year – the highest rate in Europe. They are not all lonely kids from care homes or run-down inner-city estates: many are from supposedly middle-class, two-parent homes in leafy suburbia. Yes, some are running away from unhappy homes, seeking 'freedom' from violent and abusive adults – knowing that having a baby will entitle them to help from the government and perhaps a room of their own. Others are just seeking 'something of my own to love'. According to the Family Planning Association, most of them 'just got carried away'. In spite of early sex education and easy access to contraceptives, few consider the future or realize the long-term problems that await them. One 15-year-old with a year-old baby said, 'Young people don't understand what a big change occurs when you become a single parent.'

An increasing number of organizations and charities are providing support for teenage mothers, teaching them parenting skills and warning them of infant health problems. In 1999, the government initiated a scheme to create a network of mother-and-baby hostels which would provide support (within a two-year limit) rather than offer lonely council tenancies. Some are already up and running, and provide practical training in childcare and in educational life skills, including budgeting. A similar initiative by the Rowan Centre in

Rotherham, funded by the local council together with a children's charity, provides full-time education and support for young mothers. From there, several of these teenagers now visit schools in their area to explain the many changes their babies have created in their lives. Like the police, they pull no punches.

'Some girls in my class envied me, but they were my friends. Our neighbours were abusive and one called me a slag.'

'The baby woke me up five times a night for the first four months.'

'When I take the baby out in his buggy, lots of old ladies come and lecture me. Some even shout out that I'm not fit to be a mother at my age.'

These messages from their peers – mostly in the form of warnings – are beginning to get across. Just as it is no use telling young people, 'Do not drink,' so they do not tell them: 'Do not become parents.' Instead, they demonstrate that everyone has a choice. 'Just remember that, and consider the consequences,' they say.

All such schemes are a far cry from the charity-run hostels of a few decades ago, where adoption was often the only choice offered for the babies of unmarried mothers. Hopefully, other local authorities, schools and charities are starting to fund such schemes. These are not restricted to girls. 'Teachers and parents seem to forget babies have fathers too,' said Alan, 17. 'We don't all disappear and leave the girls to play the mum. We need lessons in it all just as much as they do.' They are even able to attend courses on childcare. And in some areas schemes are starting up to give advice and training to help young single fathers – a small but significant group who need to be told more about their rights as well as their responsibilities.

For parents, this is not a time for misplaced prejudice. Your teenagers are not necessarily rejecting your moral codes. Don't back away from them and risk losing the love of a grandchild. They are all going to need your love and support.

The transition from adolescence to adulthood

The years between 17 and 20 can be especially full of emotions. To fail an exam or lose a boyfriend can be highly traumatic. They spend time wanting to stay within their familiar peer group, yet admire those who dare to be different; they long to be independent, yet are still afraid of too much responsibility. It is a time of great change, a sort of prolonged period of transition.

So do the 'Troublesome Teen' years come to an end when they turn 20? Some parents say they don't end until the teenagers leave home. Teenagers say it is when they get their first job, start commuting, begin learning to make ends meet. 'That made me feel grown-up!'

For parents, it is important that they themselves continue to live full lives and never let the 'empty nest' syndrome depress them. It is not always easy – many say they feel guilty when relief creeps in once the children have gone. Others can't stop worrying. However, if parents have helped their children to build up inner resources throughout the years to cope with changes, they can rest assured that their youngsters will survive. For the teenagers, it is not always as easy as they imagine it will be – but once they stop feeling possessed by the parents, and become their friends, the transition period will be over.

7

Disability or Ill Health in the Family

'What a change in our house when my brother had his accident – he was in a wheelchair for ages.'

A change indeed – as anyone will understand who has experienced any form of disability in a member of their family. That young boy, whose elder brother was paralysed in a car accident, appreciated that his life, as well as that of his brother, was going to be different from now on. He couldn't walk to school with him, or play football at weekends. Their mother was so taken up with her injured son that she had little time for anything else. It took many months for them all to adjust to their altered lives.

Today the medical and social help that is available for children is improving all the time – the rehabilitation as well as the physical care they receive is brilliant. But what of the able-bodied, healthy children who live or go to school with them? Are they being helped to understand how much *they* can do to help others who are not so fortunate?

Through organizations such as the Child-to-Child Trust, and from information within their schools, young people are being made aware of the parts they can play in a disabled person's life. As a Trust adviser writes: 'Attitudes are crucial.' Gone are the days when to have a physically or mentally disabled child was considered almost shameful – he or she might be handed over to an institution, be 'hidden away'. Now, mainstream schools not only accept but encourage all children into their classrooms.

In a primary school that offers Sign Support Service, the deaf children are able to take part in all the activities. The other children all learn to sign, and are able to talk with their deaf schoolmates quite naturally. A specialist teacher will sit with the deaf children to interpret any instructions they might miss, and so they are included in all the lessons – and the tickings off! At other schools I've seen several children using walking frames who are also treated the same as everyone else – there's seldom any unkind teasing.

So how can a child come to terms with the changes that his sibling's disability will engender? There are a growing number of disability information and mental health services throughout Britain. The advice from their specialists and teachers is basically: be friendly, play with your brother or sister. Don't just think of them as being different, think of them as special – acknowledge that they may have skills or talents that you don't have. 'My sister's partially sighted, but she's way ahead of me in maths,' boasted Mark, aged 11.

One nine-year-old boy knew there was something 'different' about his brother who wasn't able to go to school. He had to be helped to dress and he ate like a baby. 'He was seven, and I had to, like, baby-sit for him. It wasn't fair.' Then one day their doctor told the boy he could help his brother to change for the better. He explained how the younger boy had an illness that didn't show – it was inside his head. 'You can teach him to dress, to eat, and perhaps make up a sign language so you can talk to each other.' To the nine-year-old's surprise, it worked. 'Now we're friends. He seems to understand me, and tries hard to do things for himself. I know he'll never be really better, but he loves me to play with him. He sure has changed!'

Children soon realize that disabled children are just like others in every way except for their disability. They are often quicker to appreciate that than adults!

However, whether a child's disablement is caused by an inherited illness or an accident, or he is born deaf or blind, this will mean a huge change for all the family.

One girl, the youngest of four sisters, was severely handicapped from birth, and has had to use a walking frame from the age of four. Every movement is difficult for her. The other girls love her dearly, but sometimes resent the special attention their sister has from their parents. 'We have to walk to school and she gets to go in the car,' grumbled one of them, while another said how they couldn't go to their favourite holiday beach because 'She can't climb down the cliff with us and Mum says it wouldn't be fair.'

Children as carers

When you hear talk of carers you imagine a parent, a spouse or a social worker. But there are many children – over 50,000 in the UK, some of them still in primary school – for whom caring for a parent or sibling, possibly both, is a regular part of their lives.

An eight-year-old girl has to look after three younger siblings as well as nurse her disabled mother. And a six-year-old is caring for her father who is an alcoholic – she checks his drinks and has taken on the responsibility of worrying over him.

When Prue was ten, her mother's MS suddenly worsened and she had to use a wheelchair. As an only child, Prue found herself having to cope with the things her mother could no longer manage. 'I had to do the hoovering and make the beds, and pick up things Mum dropped, fetch things for her, and sometimes push her down to the shops.' Although a local support group provided help during the day while the child was at school, her father was never home from work until late in the evening, so she had to cook an evening meal and help her mother get ready for bed. 'Luckily Mum got an electric wheelchair this year,' said Prue, now 14, 'so she can get about on her own. She can press the buttons on the chair to move it around, but she can't write very well, so I write letters for her. Sometimes it's hard to find time to do all my homework.'

I suggested her life really had changed dramatically. 'Yes, I suppose it has. Mum used to drive me to school, now I have to go on the bus. Sometimes I get to go on a holiday with her which is organized by a disabled organization – which is good, but not the same as when we could go where we wanted. Dad has left us now, though he keeps in touch.' A sad story, told briefly by a very modest, but still very young, carer.

When Sylvia and Shirley's mother died, they were only 11 and 13, and they were approached by a local young carers' support group. Their father wondered if this was necessary. 'Surely I'm the carer?' he asked. But the two children found they were indeed having to care for their dad. 'We sort of feel responsible for him, he misses Mum so much – he wouldn't bother to eat much if we didn't go to the supermarket for him, he'd rather just have a drink,' said Sylvia. Their caring is not as demanding as it is for Prue, but it is a sort of anxiety for them – they are both old for their years, and want to care for their father 'in case he gets ill or something, like Mum, then we'd be left on our own'.

Those two girls at least have each other, but some young carers do need their support groups. They may be close to a parent they care for, but are not always able to talk openly to them about their problems. 'Mum doesn't want to hear my worries,' said Prue, 'and when I do see Dad he doesn't really listen to me.' As we have seen, adolescence is hard enough without any added difficulties.

Debbie badly needed to be listened to when she was at school. Her mother is severely disabled with arthritis and her only sister has asthma. 'I'm always, like, wondering how Mum is. But when I tried to ring her on my mobile phone, my teacher took it away. She didn't understand that Mum sometimes falls on the stairs and gets paralysed. I worry all the time. At home I can look after her, do the housework and the cooking and shopping.' Debbie's school friends couldn't understand why she would never go out with them, and began to bully her and then to ignore her. 'We were afraid to tell anyone as Mum thought the Social Services might come and put her into a home.' (This is a constant worry among carers, and the reason so many families hide their problems.) Only when a young carers group heard about Debbie's family did the school get to know the truth, and now Debbie feels far more relaxed. 'I still worry, but my class teacher is very kind to me and my friends understand me at last. They know I can't always go out with them, to the cinema or something, but it's good to be asked.'

Many children, like Debbie, find that caring takes up so much of their time that their lives become increasingly lonely. Nina's mother is also in a wheelchair. 'I can never go out, and can't ask my friends round. I have to cook the meals, make lunch boxes for my little sister and me, as well as doing the housework – you know, washing and ironing and so on. I worry about Mum a lot, and don't want her to worry about us – so when I get letters from school about outings and so on, I never give them to her. She is so often in pain – and very brave. But my littlest sister cries and says she'd rather have a proper mum. I wish I had someone to talk to.'

Martin, only 12 years old, has to help care for his granny. 'Mum has long hours at work and my little brother is only six, and he's not too well anyway so can't do much. So I have to shop for Nan and push her in her wheelchair to the hospital for treatment quite a lot. I often cook for the family – Mum sometimes has to work nights. But she is very kind – after all, a mum is the only person you really need.'

The Children's Society writes of the 'psychological, social and emotional cost' to young carers for all the work they do. They take on, often on their own initiative, so much responsibility, which can affect their schooling. 'I got told off for daydreaming,' said one young boy, 'but I was worried about Dad who was on some new medication and I hoped he could manage until I got home.'

The Princess Royal Trust for Carers (see Sources of Help, p. 91) found that a high percentage of teachers are not aware which of their pupils are carers, and also that these children are often bullied. Nina was badly teased for not asking her friends home. 'I can't because Mum finds extra noise in the house too stressful. It makes me feel sort of excluded at school.'

Racism combined with such exclusion often makes young black carers doubly stressed. Their caring responsibilities can be less formal than their white peers, and consequently erratic school attendance leads to few, if any, educational qualifications. Their future job prospects are put in jeopardy.

Not surprisingly, stress levels are high among many of these children, often unable to see beyond their present problems. One young boy is touchingly loyal towards his brother, who is autistic. 'Yes, he does horrid things to me, like messing up my bedroom and breaking my computer, and he runs off when Mum's at work and I'm meant to be watching him. But I get mad when people in the street stare at him and say he's retarded. I love him because he's my brother, but what will happen when we grow up? I guess he'll have to live with me.'

Since the Carers [Recognition and Services] Act 1995, the needs of all young carers are becoming more widely recognized, and the number of young carers groups around the UK is growing year by year. Now many more of these young people are able to meet others in the same position as themselves and have a chance to go on trips and outings and 'have fun like normal families'. More importantly, it is understood that they all need emotional as well as physical support. As we have seen, the children are constantly anxious about their disabled or sick parent or sibling – and this can have a major impact on their lives. 'My brother is 19 now and yet has the intelligence of a child of about eight,' says Liz-Anne. 'I'm 13 now and get embarrassed when I'm out with this tall young man who plays with toys! Yet my main worry is what will happen when I have to go out to work and can't look after him any more. Mum is disabled, so it is a worry for her, too.'

The 1995 Act's legal definition of young carers is: 'Children and young people (under 18) who provide or intend to provide a substantial amount of care on a regular basis'. However, a young carer has added a corollary: 'This does not really describe what it is like for us and our families – although we share common experiences with other young carers, we are all individual with different needs and lifestyles.'

Happily, the young carers groups are acknowledging these differences and enabling many of the families to have outings together 'rather than isolating the disabled'. They all want to be 'as normal as possible' and to be able to face the future with hope rather than fear. And many of them are indeed wonderfully well-adjusted youngsters, most of them capable far beyond their years. Hopefully the groups will be able to prevent too many of them suffering any psychological effects in their adult lives. 'I come once a week to my group, and it has changed my outlook completely. I've been on two trips with them and made some new friends. They let us have fun, and are interested when we talk to them.'

What all young carers need is to be trusted, respected and, above all, listened to, by the adults around them.

Hospice care

One place where children are always listened to is a hospice. Here, where the pervading atmosphere is of caring, no one is allowed to feel a burden to anyone else. Dame Cecily Saunders, founder of the Hospice Movement, advocated that whatever the age of the terminally ill child, she has a 'climate of security'.

The nurses and social workers take special interest in the visiting brothers and sisters of siblings who are dying – they know them all by name. If anyone can restore self-esteem to a child, they can.

A lively little girl called Megan found it hard to understand how her ten-year-old brother could suddenly become so weak and frail. He used to tease her, push her around, and generally be the typical boisterous brother, and now he was in a wheelchair. 'Our family life just isn't the same any more since Danny got ill,' she cried, 'and now they're taking him to a hospice, it's awful!' Only when one of the nurses spoke with her, played games with her beside her brother's bed, and helped her parents to tell her the truth, did she begin to accept the huge change in her young life.

'When my sister was taken to the hospice I was jealous,' admitted Ben, aged 11. 'Nothing was the same at home. Mum was never there to get our meals, Dad was never free to help with homework, it was horrible.' Then Ben's grandmother took him along to the hospice one day after school. 'I dreaded it,' he said, 'I knew hospitals were places where you go in and don't come out. But it wasn't like a hospital, the doctors didn't even wear white coats! They talked to me like a grown-up and told me all about my sister's illness – one of them even asked *me* some questions about her. I felt really included. It was great.' Even after his sister had died, the hospice staff kept in touch with Ben and his parents. 'I knew our home life would change, but the nurses made me feel Mum and Dad did care about me after all.'

A hospice social worker summed up such stories: 'Families often don't talk enough among themselves. They bring in a child who is desperately ill, and present him or her as the *only* one in the family with a problem.' When a child has a life-limiting illness, it is of course a huge strain on any family. They know there is no cure, but the hospice offers wonderful palliative care. As a hospice therapist says, 'What you have to tell the family is that the condition *can* be managed. Yes, it is frightening, but it's all right.' And in turn the parents must tell a sick child what a hospice is – that it is a place where they will be not be made well, but will be offered care, great help and support. For older children, it is important that they are told what is happening to them – that they understand the process. For example, chemotherapy is even more awful if a child doesn't know what it is for. It is far less frightening when it is explained to you. Most appear to love coming to a hospice, and they all make many friends. The atmosphere is of a friendly home, peaceful and yet never dull.

There are now sibling support groups in several hospices for children, and they usually provide special play areas for them to relax in. How different from the days of dreary, overcrowded waiting rooms and no children under 12 being allowed into the wards! A play therapist spoke of the help such groups can give to the children and their parents.

We do offer formal play therapy if and when children need it –

we have to be able to identify those children who are struggling and would benefit from our help. But perhaps the main element in our services is helping families to understand that children need information. Even little ones know when something is wrong with a brother or sister, and need to be told the truth. We encourage parents to be honest – to give the truth in bite-size pieces to start with, and as the child grows in understanding, to fill in more detailed information. Sometimes a child doesn't talk about his own worries as he is concerned that his parents are stressed and he doesn't want to add to their worries.

Such mature concerns for a small child! Many of them, like the young carers, often act like adults when discussing their sick brother or sister. They are usually extremely caring. A little girl of eight had severe disabilities, and her twin sisters, although only four years old, were very patient. They instinctively understood that she had to have more attention from their mother than they did.

Margaret, now 11, has a young brother, Richard, who became ill with severe fitting when only six months old. He is now profoundly disabled, and Margaret has grown mature far beyond her years ('11 going on 25!' laugh her parents). One day when the ambulance had to be called to Richard, Margaret was the one who volunteered all the necessary information for the paramedics. She knew every detail of her brother's condition, all about his fits and how long they lasted, all the facts they needed. And they listened to her. Afterwards, she said that was what she appreciated. 'They listened to me!'

Margaret never neglected her brother. At her own birthday party, she insisted that Richard joined in all the games. Her friends helped him to be wheeled around even during the games of catch. Only once has the girl been known to show any anger – any frustration. That was when she heard some children bullying her brother, calling him rude names. She turned on the bullies, attacking them in no uncertain terms. She would protect him, no matter what.

However, the therapists know that even when a child shows such maturity – and many do when a sibling is terminally ill – they *are* still children, and need to be cared for themselves. If they do have feelings of resentment, which of course they do at times – just as young Ben did – they then feel guilty. Again, the nurses and therapists can reassure them that such feelings are normal.

Occasionally a child is relieved when a sibling dies – the long days and nights of anxiety, of longing for a life away from the hospice, of missing the full attention of your parents, have all been overwhelming. But then guilt comes in: surely you shouldn't be feeling glad? This is something that must be picked up by adults so that the child can be told relief is a very normal reaction, and that his feelings are OK, that of course they do not mean that you wished your sibling to die.

Support from a hospice does not stop when a child has died. Even after a terminal illness, death comes as a shock. Family life changes once more. After months, perhaps years, when your home was always full of so many professionals – nurses, therapists and health visitors coming and going – it is now quiet, almost silent. This is a huge loss. But the therapist or social worker continues to work with the family, visiting the home, just as they did with young Ben, sometimes taking the siblings out for a walk or shopping. They always keep in touch, and of course offer post-bereavement support. Scott was only six when his baby brother died nearly two years ago, but the hospice therapist is only now preparing him for her visits to end. She has helped him to understand that they must finally say goodbye, but that she will stay in touch. 'After all,' she reminds his parents, 'Scott's concept of death will inevitably change as he gets older, and he will begin to ask more difficult questions.'

As we saw in Chapter 4, children do ask *very* difficult questions! And the therapists have to be aware of the answers the parents are providing, and know their beliefs. They must never confuse a child with differing theories. A small child's fantasies are often bizarre enough without confusing them further. It is never wise to underestimate the impact of death in a family. Even when they are at the pre-verbal stage, perhaps under two years old, children will feel the significance of a death, of an absence.

You can never assume a child has fully grasped the concept of death being a permanent state. A little girl who appeared to have accepted that her sister had gone to Heaven was taken to visit the small grave. But when it was suggested the grass around the grave be cut, she cried. 'No, no, you'll hurt Natalie!'

Siblings seem to worry about the pain their brother or sister may be suffering, whereas the sick child worries more about his parents – how will they cope? Whatever their circumstances, children who

73

suffer from, or witness, a progressively degenerative illness always demonstrate great strength and ability to care. 'Tragic as it was,' said one mother, 'the experience helped my children to grow and mature.'

8
Family Traumas

Some of the changes in many – far too many – children's lives are devastating. They not only destroy any hope of a normal childhood, but can have profound effects on their future adulthood. Sadly, the most serious of these changes are often caused by parental neglect. In many families, a sort of role reversal takes place: rather than parents watching out for their children's alcohol or drug abuse, many youngsters are trying to cope with such abuses or addictions among their parents.

Alcohol abuse

Picture a family of father, mother and three children living contentedly in a small town, well liked by all the neighbours, always joining in all the local events. The eldest daughter can tell you what happened:

> I suppose it was gradual, but our lives seemed to change within a few months. Dad would stay out late most nights, then when he came home he would be angry with Mum and she would cry. They would argue and we thought they might be getting divorced, but Mum said there was nothing to worry about. I don't know why she lied to us; we knew something was very wrong. Dad became violent at times, and Mum said he was ill, but by then we knew what the trouble was. He lost his job, and my brothers and I had to get paper rounds and weekend work to buy groceries. Life was never the same again.

Rachel was another mother who thought her children didn't know what was going on.

> My girls were six and nine when their father became an alcoholic and I truly thought they were unaware of any trouble, that I could hide it from them. Then after about three years the situation got worse – I was a nurse and knew it was a medical problem, but my husband had been such a loving person, I sort of denied it. But he

changed so much – I began to realize how close love is to hate. I think the children felt that too at times. And I know they felt shame, too, and guilt – because they stopped bringing their friends home. In between bouts of violence my husband would be full of remorse and regret, and get angry with himself. It was a highly damaging, emotional situation. I kept saying I would leave him, but then I didn't – so the children had no stability in their lives.

Like many others, Rachel never talked it over with her girls – even when they became teenagers. 'I never mentioned it to my parents either,' she said. 'Somehow my daughters sensed this, and never said a word to their grandparents. There we were – all in our isolated little lives – so sad.' Understandably, the girls all left home quite young – they found it more relaxing to keep in touch by phone. 'But if we asked to speak to Dad, Mum would say, "Dad is resting" or "Dad is out." We knew what that meant.'

Rachel finally joined an Al-Anon family group, a charity which provides understanding, strength and hope to anyone whose life is, or has been, deeply affected by someone else's drinking. 'The average family doctor is not always much help; they just say cut down on the drink – or never take more than three! But it is the first drink, not the last, that does the damage. Abstinence is the only cure.'

Clare also had to find help from a family group, although she and her four sons were always able to talk freely with each other. When the youngest boy was only two, her husband was left some money which coincided with him losing his job. He started drinking heavily, would be up all night, falling asleep in a chair with a cigarette burning. When he needed money for drink, he would raid the boys' piggy-banks, he was that desperate. This made the boys angry, and they became aggressive. Then he stole from the local sports club – helped himself to some raffle money. 'It was such a disgrace to us all – shaming for a long while.'

When the boys were 10, 14, 16 and 18, Clare managed to take them for a holiday.

It was a tiny rented cottage. We had no money so we watched videos all day, and I suddenly realized the boys were laughing – something they never did at home. We talked about it and all decided that we would lock Dad out of the house next time he went drinking. But he broke a window to get in, and when the boys put bolts on the doors he would kick them down – they were all very scared. They would hide the bottles of drink, and my youngest, then aged ten, stole his dad's house keys! The others piled his clothes outside, putting a towel over them as it was raining.

Clare could be proud of her sons – for when her husband took her to court to get access to them, the day before the hearing they all wrote letters to the judge telling him how very scared they were. 'My eldest boy had a nervous breakdown from fear and lack of confidence. They all need a dad; it is so sad. They know he's ill, but they look so unhappy. It is like having a hole in your heart – you feel it yourself and try not to cry. At least my sons all live at home – we are still very close. But I would never have wished such a childhood on them – full of trauma and change, nothing stable. My husband won't give me a divorce, but I can't cry; he's not dead, though his personality has changed so much he is not the man I married. I feel very isolated. Many people remember him as a happy person, but they just don't understand.'

Such dramatic changes in children's lives are hard indeed. As happens in the aftermath of bereavement or divorce, the surviving parent finds her own grief so overwhelming that she is not always able to help her children. Once again, it is the family who can talk openly among themselves who will be the better equipped to cope.

But just as the alcoholic can be helped by joining Alcoholics Anonymous (AA) and their partner can find fellow sufferers at an Al-Anon family group to talk with, so teenage children can be tremendously helped by Alateen. In one of these groups they will find others who can share their feelings and emotions. For however sympathetic friends and relations may be, those who have had similar experiences will be the ones with the greatest understanding. They will find they are not alone in their trouble, and will learn how to find a positive side to their lives.

It was many years before Joan found any help. Her mother was an alcoholic, but she found she had more trouble getting along with her non-alcoholic father.

At first I didn't realize how badly affected he was – he changed my life more than my mother as he was so full of self-pity. I did badly at school and the teachers got fed up with me. I became depressed – so much so that I tried to cut my wrists one day and was sent to hospital. This sobered Mum up a little, but Dad got even more upset because he thought I was also going to become an alcoholic. It wasn't until I was 16 that I found help from Alateen. The great thing about it was being with other kids who had the same problem, and they truly understood how I felt. I even managed to persuade Mum to go to AA and somehow we have all stayed together. But in no way are we the same family I knew as a small child.

Certainly, it is when the mother of the family is an alcoholic that more problems can arise for her children. Sandra's story is a classic example:

It was when our brother was about three that we noticed a change in our mum. She used to be such fun, always laughing, and she loved parties – but I suppose she loved them too much. She often stayed up very late and told us to put ourselves to bed. And she became more and more sort of distant – she forgot to go shopping, and when she did she bought mostly bottles of drink. The thought of Dad going off to work and leaving us with Mum makes me wonder how we all survived. It seemed to happen suddenly – we sort of became her carers instead of her looking after us. Of course, we noticed she drank a lot, and would help her to hide the empty bottles before Dad came home. My sister and I often had to do the cooking as Mum would fall asleep by lunchtime. It was only when our auntie came to stay, persuaded Mum to get help, and introduced us to Alateen that life became almost normal.

Maria and her family owe a great deal to the two family groups who provide support and fellowship for those with the common problem of alcoholism.

My husband has had a drink problem since childhood. But we never discussed it as a family. We sort of kept it a secret – at least, I did, as I was ashamed of him and wondered what people would think of me. I used threats, crying, pouring drink away – all the classic attempts to cure him – of course to no avail. When our only son was 15 we all went to an alcohol and drug unit in our town. We went daily, and were offered weekly sessions as a family. After all, I now know it does affect the whole family. But the most painful thing I discovered was that it was *my* behaviour that affected my son. My husband did appalling things. He would take our son out in his car, they went off for sort of 'boys together' days as we live in the country, but they always came home via a pub. He would buy our son a lemonade. I would nag and moan when they came home late for lunch, I was full of anger. Looking back, a lot of the worry was my own fault. I allowed my son to go in the car with his dad as I fooled myself into thinking that with his son there he wouldn't drink, but of course he did. I tried very hard to make my son despise his father like I did, but he only became more drawn towards his dad.

When our son was very little, I was a normal mum, though I hadn't many friends because of my husband's drinking. I would be watching from 6 p.m. for him to come home, afraid the neighbours would see him, and worried that he would have an accident after drinking at the pub. He always called there on the way home, he never drank at home. When he arrived home, I started to get grumpy and took my anger out on my son – put him to bed in a bad temper, running his dad down all the while.

Looking back, I was always angry – when we went to school concerts I was afraid my husband might fall off his chair, would disgrace my son. Only years later I learned that all the boys would have bets on which dad went to sleep first, and also which mum had the worst temper! At one time, my husband wanted to stop, to call AA, and I wouldn't let him – I was ashamed. He lost his job. I still despised him even when he was getting better very fast. I just kept thinking, what about me? I thought I was keeping us all together, but I was a real pain in the end. I was the violent one, not my husband. I know now how much I hurt our son, for I was full of frustration as his dad was not there to deal with him. I was never physically violent towards him, but verbally I was abusive towards both of them. Only when my husband went to AA, and I went to Al-Anon and our son to Alateen, did I discover that I was the one upsetting our son, not my husband. I learned also what my son really thought of me.

Maria's son has his say:

> While Dad was drinking, life was normal. He worked hard, took me out a lot, we did boys' things together, and at the group we were told that there would be a magical change in behaviour when the drinking stopped. But when Dad stopped there was no support from any of the fellowships. That was when I was affected most, and I was really scared. Only when we all found help did I learn why Dad drank, why Mum acted as she did, and where I fitted into all of it.

This young boy was fortunate in finally getting help. Too often, a child who has suffered such a childhood can carry a great deal of anxiety and unresolved anger well into his adulthood.

Maria now knows that it was her behaviour that did the most damage in her son's young life. She continued:

> Our son left home to join the Army before he was 18, and whenever he phoned me I would ask if he was phoning from a pub, and when he came home on leave I would ask him how much all the other soldiers drank. I suppose I was scared it was hereditary. But one time when he came home he laughed and said, 'Well done, you've not asked me about the pub this time!' It made me realize what I was doing to him. And what I had done to his childhood.

Drug abuse

> My brother used to steal money and CDs from my room, and once he took my watch. I didn't realize at first that it was to buy drugs. I was about 13 then and looked up to him as he was five years older than me. But he began to change – he was full of beans one minute and then angry and rude the next – and hung out with the worst gang at school. Mum and Dad changed, too. That was worse, in a way – they talked about nothing else and even when I was taking my GCSEs they just went on and on about Geoff. I seriously began to wonder if I should take drugs too, so they'd notice me.

Young lives do change dramatically when any member of a family becomes a drug user. And, sadly, it is the whole family that is affected. As many family counsellors stress, it is often outsiders who are the most judgmental. 'Neighbours can brand a whole family with the stigma when one child is an abuser. Even teachers have been heard to refer to a pupil as being "that lad from the drug family". Siblings come in for a lot of stick – as though they aren't suffering enough.'

When she was still in primary school, Liz began to worry about her father, who was always disappearing for a few days and when home would often verbally abuse her mother. She was an only child and felt her role was to protect her mother – but she soon realized that her mother took drugs. It was several years before she understood her father's behaviour was a mixture of fear and shame – how could his wife behave like this? Because her father was unable to face reality and get professional help, Liz had to look after him as well as run the house for her mother, cook all the meals and do the washing. Psychologists stress that the healthy development of any child who is struggling to adapt to what her parents want will suffer, as she will have little energy left to concentrate on her own growing up. Poor Liz never even had the support that child carers so readily deserve, as we saw in Chapter 7.

Parental imprisonment

Drug abuse is only one of many causes for a prison sentence. When a child sees a parent or sibling taken away, he will often suffer more than the offender himself.

Researchers tell us that over 100,000 children see their fathers sent to prison every year in England and Wales. The consequent changes in those children's lives are traumatic – affecting their emotional, social and educational lives.

For one family, when their violent and abusive father was imprisoned for ten years it was a relief – and there may well be many families whose reactions are similar. Likewise, release from prison of a parent may not always be something to look forward to. When 14-year-old Mick's father went to prison, Mick was only seven. He is very apprehensive about seeing him again. 'I know he used to steal money to buy drugs, and I'm scared he might start again, but I'm glad we don't have to visit the prison any more.'

Jenny, now nearly ten, has also become quite philosophical about all the traumatic changes in her life. Her father – a violent, abusive (though not to Jenny) alcoholic – had finally forced her mother to leave their home, taking the child with her. 'We moved so often I've lost count of the schools I've been to. When Mum was in the women's refuge they sent me to a school with some other refuge kids – it was all right, but I didn't learn much.' With her father now in prison, Jenny is, for the first time, in a school she enjoys. 'It's the best school I've ever been to,' she said, then added, 'and Mum and I are together, that's all that matters.' Pathetically old for her years, Jenny is of course behind academically, but has always been able to talk with her mother. The truth has never been hidden from her. She will be well equipped to face the changes her life will inevitably continue to bring.

When 14-year-old Anna's father was given a three-year prison sentence for burglary, her mother was quite unable to cope with Anna and her younger sister. 'Mum takes drugs and sometimes we have to go with her to get her fix. If Dad was here at least he could, like, give me some money to buy food. I often can't go to school as Mum needs me. Three years seems like a long time.'

Luke was hoping his stepfather would get sent back to prison. 'He was inside for quite a few years for killing someone, and I don't trust him. Mum don't care so long as he takes her to the pub every night.'

But for many children, the sudden departure of a dad they love is as grievous as a bereavement. It is a sad fact, however, that where a bereaved child will be comforted, the child of an imprisoned criminal is offered no such support. Many former friends in his peer group will now ignore him, call him names, perhaps start bullying. It is left to a shocked and anxious mother to explain to her children what is happening. Some are too upset to give much attention to their families – they may even lie to them, 'Dad may be away for a while.' A classic example of: *if you want to help a child, help his parent first.*

But what if it is a single parent who is imprisoned? Or if, as does happen, both parents are sentenced? Health visitors, probation officers and social workers are not always available to give the support, guidance or even financial aid to the children left behind who are suffering such tragic, unintended punishment. 'When they sent us into care it was sort of like they were sending us to prison as well as Mum and Dad!'

Reactions to the whole drama are usually varied – often similar to those following a loss through death or divorce – and include shock, anger, guilt, depression and despair. A child's behaviour will always be disturbed: some will refuse school or even run away from home, others may retreat into themselves. As we have seen in the last chapter, children often cope wonderfully well with their parents' problems and addictions, and give them tremendously loyal support. They deserve far greater assistance than they presently receive from local authorities, who are currently struggling in many areas with the growing number of these innocent victims of crime.

Teachers, especially in primary schools, are often the only adults in a child's life with whom she is able to talk. More than once, in the middle of a classroom lesson, a child has whispered to me, 'Dad is in prison' or 'My brother is in court again.' Teachers should always be told about such children – as they are when a family death or separation has happened. A child doesn't want it shouted out aloud, but is relieved when a teacher is able to listen to her, perhaps to allay her fears and fantasies.

Maybe the changes in lifestyle for these children, such as a smaller home, Mum working longer hours, Granny 'taking sides', are the same as those following other losses, but now few friends will rally round to help. Sometimes the children are branded as criminals by thoughtless neighbours, and loneliness and fear may become overwhelming.

9

Changing for the Better

Every chapter so far has told of changes and losses – all our lives are full of them. And we accept them, and help our children to accept them, if we see them all as normal, natural and necessary. However, we must never forget that many changes do turn out for the better – even those we dread, or challenge, or complain about.

Unexpected happiness

Josh complained bitterly when his life was changed dramatically as ill health forced him to leave the farming life he had struggled to achieve. 'I'd always wanted to farm, and the wide open spaces of Australia appealed to me rather than a smallholding in England.' Leaving school at 15, it took Josh nearly two years to earn enough money for a flight. When he finally arrived he found his dream farm, thousands of acres of wheat, and a friendly farmer who gave him work and a roof over his head. He was blissfully happy. Then he became ill – a seemingly mysterious virus – which eventually was diagnosed as an allergy to the spray used on the crops. Sheep farming didn't appeal to him, and reluctantly he looked for work around the outskirts of Sydney. The first job he found was helping at a fish restaurant, which he hated, but it was right on the coast and this gave him the idea of working with boats. 'I was naïve, knew nothing about the sea, but I got an evening job cleaning the decks of some rich guy's huge motor cruisers. It's a long story, but I worked hard, learned to navigate, and got to buy a small craft, hired it out and then started to teach children how to sail! Yes, me, the farmer!' Josh discovered he loved boats and loved children, and now runs his own little company. He is once again blissfully happy. 'When I had to change from farming, I was so depressed and could see no future. Now I know that awful allergy was the best thing that ever happened to me!'

Happy families

Vicky had never known her father, who had died when she was a baby, and she and her mother were very close. When she was nine, her mother told her that she was about to get married. Immediately Vicky became almost numb with depression – and fear. She would lose her mum, she would have a cruel stepfather, she would never be happy again! No way would she be a willing bridesmaid at the wedding, no way would she drink a toast at the party afterwards. 'What is there to celebrate?' she asked loudly. But the 'cruel' stepfather, Alan, was one of those men born to be fathers. He did nothing to disrupt Vicky's normal routine, but let her choose where they would go for a summer holiday and quietly helped them around the house and garden. After about a year, Vicky's grand-mother asked her how she was getting on with Alan. 'Oh, he's great!' the child replied. Asked if she would rather go back to living just with her mother, she added, 'No, Gran. Life has changed so much – I never thought it could be so good. Mum is happy too. It makes our old life together look quite dull – we seem to laugh more now.'

When William's mother remarried he was also not too pleased, although he was only five and had just started school. His dad had left them to live in America, but he still remembered him and sometimes spoke to him on the phone. He didn't really want another man around – it made him feel sort of angry inside. But this new man brought another little boy aged six with him, and it was quite fun having a sort of brother to play with. 'Then Mum had another baby, and we felt more of a family.' A happy story – and one that is not unusual – though of a kind that seldom gets talked about.

'Our dad's working!'

In spite of benefits and welfare systems, many families still struggle to house, feed and clothe their children. Sean, Phil and Rhonda's dad had been out of work for over five years. 'We weren't ever really hungry,' said Sean, now 15. 'But we never had treats like other kids at school, and of course never went on holiday or anything. Mum couldn't go out to work as she couldn't afford a baby-sitter for Rhonda, and she did ironing – there was always a great pile of other people's clothes in our back room. My brother sometimes tried some of them on – he was fed up always having my old ones.' It all sounded like Victorian times, but their mum said it was all true. 'But when Dad suddenly got a job again the change was incredible. Oh, we couldn't have everything we wanted, like, but it was great to have some extra food, and I got some new football boots. But the biggest change was in Mum and Dad – they looked younger somehow! Like, they didn't shout at us so much. Life is sure much better now.'

It was a similar happy change for a family in Scotland – two girls of ten and 12, and twin boys of seven. Their dad had been in prison for four years and they only got to visit him once a year as it was too expensive for them all to travel that far. 'We were sorry for Dad – I mean, he hadn't hurt anyone or anything, just sort of borrowed some money that he wasn't supposed to or something,' said one of the girls. But even so, they were all afraid of him coming home. 'Suppose he had changed – suppose he had turned into a criminal or something.' Even the eldest girl was a bit scared. 'But he had fixed up to go and work on a farm. What a change! It was hard at first, but then we all found out what a super dad we had – he really loved us and our lives are quite different now.'

'I've found a happy home at last!'

The change in Naomi's life was traumatic and looked all set to cause her great unhappiness. When her mother died, she was sent to a foster home. She was eight at the time, and inconsolable. Her father never visited her, and although her foster parents were kind she never felt at home. She became so depressed that she was moved to another home, and then another, but after a year she had regressed into a sullen, silent child. 'I used to beg to be moved, then when I was moved I would cry,' she says. 'I just knew that wherever I was sent felt wrong.' Then after another year she was sent to a foster mother in quite another part of the county – which meant a new school also. Surely that would spell disaster? 'But when I walked into the house, the mother came to meet me and I felt quite different. The family seemed to be right for me – and they accepted me. It was amazing. One of their girls went to school with me and I loved it.' Naomi has never looked back. 'You never can tell which changes are going to work for the better,' she says. 'But when they do, it's like you can almost forget the bad things!'

Changes and surprises

Adrian had a wonderfully upbeat tale to tell. When asked if he recalled any changes in his childhood, he laughed. 'Every day!' was his answer, and he explained: 'Dad and Mum had a second-hand shop. You know, they had all the things you have in a house – furniture and rugs and other stuff, all sorts. It wasn't just a question of living above the shop, we lived *in* it, really! And I never knew what might be in our house each afternoon when I got back from school. More than once my bed was gone! When I was younger I was a bit upset sometimes as my favourite toy would disappear – anything could go. Most times the changes were good, though: we sometimes got a super new rug or a desk or something. I don't suppose Dad made a lot of money, but he was always laughing, he was happy.' Adrian laughed a lot himself. 'Was it a life of changes? More like a life of surprises, really!'

Where there is hope . . .

There are children for whom almost any change in their lives would surely be for the better – they have reached a numbing stage of hopelessness. For them, the words 'hope', 'expectation' and 'trust' are meaningless.

How do you tell if your parents are high? What do you do if your father tries to force you into burglary? What do you do if your younger brothers and sisters are starving? How do you cope if your mother wants to sell you to pay for her drugs? Their lives inspire rage in them, they live on the streets and dare not trust anyone, or each other. 'You never know who might stab you in the back.' But their numbers are such that they live in a pack, and if an outsider tried to hurt one of them the others would turn to and help.

All this is happening in the streets of far too many of our inner cities in Europe and around the world. But for one small group there is an escape route for such children – a charity called Kids Company at The Arches in central London. As the name suggests, this project is based in six railway arches where up to 500 children on any one day, who have been physically, mentally or sexually abused, can find sanctuary.

The Company, which has been running since 1996, was the

brainchild of Camila Batmangheldjh, a psychotherapist, a wonderfully dedicated lady who believes passionately in the potential of every one of the profoundly vulnerable children who refer themselves to Kids Company. 'As a service we have taken on board the reality of children who are not being parented, as well as children whose carers actively traumatize them.' Her understanding of, and genuine love for, every one of the young people is heart-warming. 'Emotional numbness,' she says, 'becomes a useful tool in protecting against the pain of trauma – but it also closes the door to positive feelings. Without appropriate help, emotionally numb children soon grow into coldness. Melting the hardness within them is vital.' Even when dealing with children involved in serious crime, Camila fully understands their lack of compassion, or of remorse. 'You can only regret causing another person pain if you are capable, empathetically, of feeling the pain you have caused to your victim ... compassion can only exist in the context of empathy.'

Camila originally set up The Place To Be, a therapeutic project in schools, highly commended by the Department of Health, which has since been widely replicated.

When the children arrive they find it impossible to believe that any adults might actually want to love or care for them, and are unable to trust or respect them. They have become desensitized to love or loyalty and have to be re-educated to understand such things exist. Younger ones think they are street-wise, but they are not really – they are in desperate need of help and need time to relax. At the Company, which they think of as their 'Club', they find much to interest them – sport, videos, a music room, arts facilities. There are also massage and reflexology sessions to relax them, and counselling sessions are always available. Understandably, these vulnerable children whose lives have been so cruelly damaged – some are refugees from war-torn countries – face endlessly complicated problems. They like not being made to work all the time at the Club and are allowed to use activities to release their creativity – they often have such pent-up rage inside them. The staff are a mixture of social workers, psychotherapists, a child psychiatrist, and sports and arts facilitators, all of whom appreciate the horrors of the circumstances these children are growing up in. 'They arrive deeply depressed, often cold and hungry. We have to reduce their stress levels and nurture them, give them time to think,' said one helper.

'We give them three good meals a day. There is no charge, and when they realize that they stop shop-lifting!'

As well as being fed, the children are offered help with clothes, school uniforms, bedding and other necessities they have never owned before. Their health is also checked, with visits to dentists and opticians. For those not in school, tuition is given, paid for by their local education authority. Staff are always on hand to assist with homework and reading. The staff are also invited into local primary schools – around fifteen schools at the time of writing. They offer therapeutic support in the form of one-to-one counselling and group work on specialist topics such as bullying or bereavement, and special needs children are given classroom support and/or extra tuition. Approximately 4,000 children a week take up these services, and teachers report positive changes within their schools – enhanced creativity and a calm approach to learning.

The young people usually continue at the project for some time, often up to two years or more. Most are self-referred. They can choose which activities they want to take part in – sports, drama or computer work – and music, singing and dancing are popular.

Claire Lanyon, whose research on the project was undertaken in association with the National Children's Bureau, sums up the positive nature of the whole project:

> Because it is unconventional in nature, it is responsive and aware of the changing needs of this extremely disadvantaged group of young people. Its informality and flexible structures allow young people lacking confidence or concentration to take advantage of the services offered at their own pace. These services are developed towards their personal needs ... in a family-like atmosphere. The staff team gives them a diverse range of adult role models to work alongside and form individual relations with.

Of course, it takes time – often nine months or more – to enable a child, especially one who has previously been excluded from school, to enter or re-enter mainstream school, though many do manage it and some even come back as helpers.

Such a change in a child's life is surely magical – certainly it is for one teenager. 'The only place I found help when I came out of prison was at this Club – I call it "Help" now.' A younger child commented, 'At The Arches we can talk, like if you have any problems, and we also can play games and they offer me some dinner. It is lovely.'

So many young lives being changed for the better. The philosophy at Kids Company promotes respect and love. It also returns to children a dignity, which is their birthright. All children deserve such love. They don't need constant advice: 'You must do this, you must do that . . .' They just need someone who cares to guide them, and to listen. That's what they do at The Arches, listen.

Children who have found such guidance, even if they have experienced countless, sometimes tragic, changes while growing up, are often those who eventually lead successful and fulfilled lives. They have learned that loss is often the price we pay for loving, and that change is part of life. Children who have been helped to understand such truths will have the strength and confidence to face whatever life throws at them.

Sources of Help

Adfam National
Waterbridge House
32–36 Loman Street
London SE1 0EE
020 7928 8900 (10 a.m.–5 p.m. Mon., Wed.–Fri.)
Helpline for the families and friends of drug users, giving confidential advice about drugs and details of local support services.

Al-Anon family groups UK and Eire
61 Great Dover Street
London SE1 4YF
020 7403 0888 (confidential helpline 10 a.m.–10 p.m. every day)
Website: www.hexnet.co.uk/alanon
Understanding and support for families and friends of problem drinkers, whether the alcoholic is still drinking or not.

Alateen
Alateen is a part of Al-Anon (scc above).
For young people aged 12–20 who have been affected by someone else's drinking, usually that of a parent.

British Agencies for Adoption and Fostering (BAAF)
Skyline House
200 Union Street
London SE1 0LX
020 7593 2041/42
Website: www.baaf.org.uk

Carers UK
Ruth Pitter House
20–25 Glasshouse Yard
London EC1A 4JT
Administration: 020 7490 8818
Direct line for young carers: 020 7566 7616
Helps carers to speak with a stronger voice. Provides information and advice on all aspects of caring. Puts young carers in touch with local groups.

Chance for Children Trust
Freepost SE6892
London SE25 4BR
020 8997 5831
Works with statutory and voluntary bodies to provide therapeutic activities such as music, art and drama to children and young people who have been through a period of trauma. Also provides support for parents and carers. Families can approach them directly.

Child and family guidance clinics
Ask your GP or local Citizens Advice Bureau for your nearest clinic.

The Childcare Link
0800 096 02 96 (Freephone)
Website: www.childcarelink.gov.uk
Information on childcare and early education options, including tips on how to pay for childcare.

The Children's Society
Edward Rudolf House
Margery Street
London WC1X 0JL
Action line: 0845 300 1128
Website: www.thechildrenssociety.org.uk
The Society offers support to children and families under pressure.

Child-to-Child Trust
Institute of Education
20 Bedford Way
London WC1H 0AL
020 7612 6649
Website: www.child-to-child.org/
A charity which can supply activity sheets for teachers and parents to help children with physical or mental disabilities.

Citizens Advice Bureaux
CAB will offer advice, useful addresses and further sources of help. Your nearest branch will be listed in the local telephone directory.

Criminal Records Bureau (CRB)
An executive agency of the Home Office
Information line: 0870 90 90 811

Cruse – Bereavement Care
Cruse House
126 Sheen Road
Richmond
Surrey TW9 1UR
020 8939 9530
Helpline: 0870 167 1677
Website: www.crusebereavementcare.org.uk

Disability Information Services for Surrey
Harrowlands
Harrowlands Park
Dorking
Surrey RH4 2RA
Enquiries: 01306 875156
The DISS network provides information on all aspects of living with disability for Surrey residents. Their enquiry line also enables those in need to locate similar resources nationwide.

Families Anonymous
Helpline: 0845 1200 660
For relatives and friends concerned about the use of drugs.

Family Rights Group (for children in care or at risk)
The Print House
18 Ashwin Street
London E8 3DL
020 7923 2628
Freephone advice line: 0800 731 1696 (1.30–3.30 p.m. weekdays)
Website: www.frg.org.uk
Expert advice on all family matters.

Gingerbread
7 Sovereign Close
Sovereign Court
London E1W 3HW
020 7488 9300
Freephone line: 0800 018 4318 (weekdays)
Website: www.gingerbread.org.uk
Offering expert advice for lone parents and children. Contact Head Office for details of nationwide groups.

Marie Stopes International
Website for 11–15-year-olds: www.likeitis.org.uk
Tel. for parents: 020 7574 7400
The family planning charity.

National Childminding Association (NCMA)
Services Manager
Northgate House
Plough Road Centre
Great Bentley
Colchester CO7 8LG
01206 252301
Website: www.ncma.org.uk
Registered charity formed to raise standards and enhance the image
and status of child minding. Can help people who wish to take up
child minding and can give advice to parents on what to look for in a
child minder.

Parentline Plus
520 Highgate Studios
53–79 Highgate Road
Kentish Town
London NW5 1TL
020 7284 5500
Free confidential helpline: 0808 800 2222
Website: www.parentlineplus.org.uk
Incorporates the National Stepfamily Association, Parent Network
and Parentline. Gives support and offers a range of leaflets on family
issues.

Pre-School Learning Alliance
National Centre
69 Kings Cross Road
London
WC1X 9LL
020 7833 0991
Website: www.pre-school.org.uk

The Princess Royal Trust for Carers
London Office
142 Minories

London EC3N 1LB
020 7480 7788
Website: www.carers.org
The Trust is in touch with a number of young carers in London and nationally.

The Sex Education Forum
8 Wakley Street
London EC1V 7QE
020 7843 6000
Send an SAE for a parents' factsheet.

The Tavistock Clinic
College Crescent
120 Belsize Lane
London NW3 5BA
020 7435 7111
NHS out-patient clinic which promotes the mental health of families. Contact the Child and Family Department (up to age 13) Mon.–Fri. For the Adolescent Department (ages 14–21) phone 020 7447 3714. Adolescents over 16 (and up to age 30) can phone or write to the Young People's Consultation Service for an appointment on 020 7447 3783. This is a self-referral service which provides a brief period of counselling (four sessions).

The Who Cares? Trust
Kemp House
152–160 City Road
London EC1V 2NP
020 7251 3117
Website: www.thewhocarestrust.org.uk
A national charity working to improve public care for children separated from their families and living in residential or foster care. Supplies educational publications for foster carers and for young people in public care.

Young Carers Initiative
The Children's Society
Youngs Yard
Finches Lane

95

Twyford
Nr. Winchester SO21 1NN
01962 711511
Website: www.childrenssociety.org.uk/youngcarers

Help from the Internet

www.itsnotyourfault.org
This provides information and practical support for young children and teenagers whose parents are divorcing or separating. There are also pages for parents, and suggested further helpful services.

www.chatdanger.com
Offers advice on what can go wrong and teaches children how to be safe online.

Further Reading

Bode, Janet, *Kids Still Having Kids*, Franklin Watts 1999

Byrne, Sheila, and Chambers, Leigh, *Joining Together*, British Agencies for Adoption and Fostering (BAAF) Publications 1998

Dowling, Emilia, and Gorell Barnes, Gill, *Working with Children and Parents through Separation and Divorce*, Macmillan 2000

Gravelle, Karen and Jennifer, *The Period Book*, Judy Piatkus 1997

Heyman, Suzie, *You Just Don't Listen Any More*, Vermilion 1998

Kitzinger, Sheila and Celia, *Talking with Children about Things that Matter*, Pandora 2000 (new edition)

Schofield, Gillian, *Growing Up in Foster Care*, BAAF Publications 2000

Willson, Andrea, *Families*, Professional Publishing 1999

Books for teenagers

Danziger, Paul, *The Divorce Express*, Hodder Children's Books 2001 (young adult)

Fine, Anne, *Flour Babies*, Puffin 1994

McBratney, Sam, *You Just Don't Listen*, Mammoth 1994

Welford, Sue, *Nowhere to Run*, Oxford University Press 1999

Welford, Sue, *The Shadow of August*, Oxford University Press 1995

Books for children

Amos, Janine, *Moving*, Cherrytree Press 1998

Anderson, Rachel, *Paper Faces*, Oxford University Press 1991 (paperback 2002) (10 years +)

Ashley, Bernard, *The Trouble with Donovan Croft*, Oxford University Press 2002 (10–12 years)

Gleitzman, Morris, *Two Weeks with the Queen*, Penguin 1989

Hanks, Kevin, *Lily's Purple Plastic Purse*, Hodder Children's Books 2002 (4–7 years)

Meyer, Donald (ed.), *Views from Our Shoes – Growing Up with a Brother or Sister with Special Needs*, Woodbine House 1997 (all ages)

Wilson, Jacqueline, *The Worry Website*, Doubleday 2002 (8–11 years)

Books to read with a child

Bryant-Mole, Karen, *What's Happening?* Wayland Publishers 1992

Foxon, Judith, *Nutmeg Gets Adopted*, BAAF Publications 2001

Foxon, Judith, *Nutmeg Gets Cross*, BAAF Publications 2002

Orritt, Barbara, *Dennis Duckling: Going into Care*, The Children's Society 1999

Thomas, Pat, *My Family's Changing*, MacDonald Young Books 1998